Instructor's Manual, Transparency Masters, and Test Bank

for

Martin, Sexton, Wagner, Gerlovich

Teaching Science for All Children

Second Edition

prepared by

Ralph Martin
Ohio University

Colleen Sexton
Ohio Department of Education

Allyn and Bacon
Boston · London · Toronto · Sydney · Tokyo · Singapore

A Viacom Company
160 Gould Street
Needham Heights, Massachusetts 02194

Internet: www.abacon.com
America Online: keyword: College Online

ISBN 0-205-19586-5

Printed in the United States of America

10 9 8 7 6 5 4 3 2 1   01 00 99 98 97 96

Table of Contents

TEACHING SCIENCE FOR ALL CHILDREN

About This Manual

This manual is divided into four parts: teaching suggestions, chapter outlines, test item bank, and transparency masters.

Teaching Suggestions are offered to you from our experiences in developing and refining the material in the text. Several practical assignments and evaluation techniques are offered for your consideration, and each has been used successfully in our own classes.

Chapter Outlines is a section that provides a capsule description of the material and conceptual intent for each chapter. The main concepts and supporting details are outlined, with references to several of the pedagogical aids (figures, tables, etc.) that you will find in the text. The content outline may be used for presentations or as lecture notes for an instructor, or as a planning guide for customizing the material. You will find several references to transparency masters in the left margin of the chapter outline. These masters are located in the last section of this manual.

The Test Item Bank contains several hundred items, separated by chapter, in many common forms: multiple choice, matching, true-false and so on. Essay items have not been included here because they have already been inserted at the end of each chapter in the text and may be used for discussion and/or examinations. The computer software that is available to accompany this manual also makes it possible to customize and to sort items electronically.

Concept Maps are provided for each chapter. You may wish to use these as transparency masters for introducing or summarizing each chapter. Also, the maps may be copied and distributed to students as study guides. Please inform your students that they should not attempt to memorize the maps. Each map represents the authors' vision about the chapter concepts and connections among and between the concepts. Encourage your students to construct their own meaning from the chapters by creating their own concept maps.

Transparency Masters that are available to support your instruction are noted in the left margin of the chapter content outline. For example, T1.0 is the "global concepts" transparency master for Chapter, 1 and T1.1 is the first transparency for material in the content outline for Chapter 1, and so on. This coding mechanism is used for each chapter. More than 150 transparency masters are located in the last section of the manual. Student Handouts (miniature transparencies) are available for each chapter to enhance note-taking and studying. The transparency masters file is available for *PowerPoint* (Macintosh). The file permits customized class presentations. Hard copy notes may be copied as hand outs for your students, or these notes may be taken from the *PowerPoint* files.

We also would like to hear about your successes and suggestions for improving these materials. Please contact us:

Ralph Martin, Ph.D.
Professor and Director, School of C&I
Ohio University
College of Education
Athens, OH 45701-2979
(614) 593-4455
martinr@ouvaxa.cats.ohiou.edu

Colleen M. Sexton, Ph.D.
State Admin. for SchoolNet Plus
Ohio Department of Education
2151 Carmack Road
Columbus, OH 43221
(614) 728-9646
IMS_Sexton@ODE.Ohio.gov

Teaching Suggestions

Several assignments and requirements have helped our university students construct their understanding about science teaching in the same spirit as the constructivist/making connections theme that permeates our text. We wish to share these with you and encourage you to give them a try. The end of each chapter also contains discussion questions and project ideas. We have provided additional ideas below.

1. **Picture of a scientist**. We ask our students to draw a picture of a scientist and we are careful not to assign the task in any way that will bias their thinking. "Stick figures with details are fine" is one reply that has dismissed the claim some students have about not being able to draw. Analysis of the details shown in their pictures helps to set an advance organizer for the material in Chapter 1. This chapter contains a report of similar exercises involving children.

2. **"Science is ..."** is another task we assign. We ask the students to complete the thought begun with these words with a couple of sentences or a brief paragraph. Reading the variety of ideas helps to reinforce the concepts in Chapter 1 and the importance of the material in the book.

3. **"Children learn ..."** is another thought we ask the students to complete. Their ideas about how children learn, particularly science, sets a strong rationale for Chapter 2. Beyond this, goals and effective teaching methods are implied for the entire course.

4. **Concept Map Homework Assignment and Video** bring the abstract ideas behind concept mapping to a more concrete level. This assignment is given after we have tried mapping through a card sort activity that we do in conjunction with Chapter 5. You might consider using the card sort activity that is described in the outline section for Chapter 5 in this instructor's manual. Basically, we construct learning packets that include a copy of a chapter from children's science textbooks, several 3x5 cards with concepts from the chapter written, and note cards for the students to write propositions. The video tape supplied as a part of this instructor's manual illustrates how to do concept mapping. The guidelines we use for the concept mapping homework assignment are given following this section on teaching suggestions. Please feel free to use it as it is.

5. **Learning Cycle Lesson Plan and Video** are also used as a homework assignment and can be coordinated with field experience teaching or peer teaching assignments. We use the assignment early in the term to judge understanding and skills regarding science concepts, planning, teaching methods, and pupil evaluation. Misunderstandings help us to plan remedial or reinforcement instruction. A planning template helps our students to manage the comprehensive type of planning required by this teaching approach. A lesson plan evaluation form helps us to provide systematic and consistent feedback to our students. A copy of each is provided. The supportive video

tape illustrates the teaching steps of our 4-E science learning cycle. The video is provided as a part of this instructor's manual package.

6. **Learning Cycle Demonstration Lesson**, otherwise known as "peer teaching," helps us to view our students' skills and understanding in a controlled environment on campus. This is the information we give them:

> You will be assigned to a contemporary science program. Select a lesson from the curriculum, modify it, and teach it to your peers by using the science learning cycle. You must also use the class evaluation form to help your peers give you written feedback about your teaching, which will help you to self-evaluate your instruction. Make copies of your lesson plan to give to members of the class. You will be evaluated on your teaching by your instructor (see "Evaluation Form"). Be certain to demonstrate **safe science**. Each lesson will be videotaped for purposes of self-evaluation. **Please provide a VHS video tape on the day you are to be video-taped.** Your only recording will be made on the tape you provide.

7. **Peer Teaching Self Analysis Paper** is a logical, systematic follow-up to the demonstration lesson. This is the information we give our students:

> The independently written assignment for this exercise is due one week after the lesson is taught and consists of a brief paper (2-3 double-spaced typewritten pages) in which you outline your paper to include these parts:
>
> 1. Description of the lesson taught
> 2. A quantitative summary of the results from the video tape and peer evaluations (include tabulations of frequencies, percentages, etc.)
> 3. Description of the strengths and weaknesses evident in your teaching
> 4. Statement of goals for your improvement of science teaching
> 5. Statement of grade (with justification) you believe is earned

A copy of the evaluation form we use to provide systematic feedback to our students follows this section of the manual.

This assignment is supported by instructor-led peer discussion after the lesson has been taught. Verbal and written feedback help the demonstration teacher to construct a reflective analysis and evaluation of the lesson. Cooperative group discussions may be organized around specific topics such as: the nature of the Exploration action, the extent to which the concept was constructed clearly during the Explanation phase, the nature and effect of the Expansion activity, teacher's personal factors, classroom management techniques, questioning techniques, adequacy of safety procedures followed, etc.

8. <u>**Science Teaching Field Experience**</u> is vital to the real-world understanding of our future teachers. The following information is given to our students:

Science Teaching Field Experience

Lab Goals:

By getting directly involved in science teaching during the preservice field experience, you:

1. will explore and try out different methods of teaching science, including the major curriculum supplements for elementary science.
2. gain experience with pupils.
3. will develop a positive attitude toward science and science teaching.
4. will develop the science knowledge, skills, and attitudes necessary to become a successful elementary science teacher.

Lab Objectives:

During the laboratory component of the science methods course you shall:

1. express confidence in preparing and presenting science concepts to elementary pupils.
2. make use of lessons from exemplary science curricula in preparing lessons, e.g., SCIS, SAPA, ESS, OBIS, Project WILD, Project Learning Tree, TOPS, etc.
3. prepare lessons that take into account the development level of the child.
4. identify and use instructional strategies that involve children in various scientific processes, e.g., observation, measurement, hypothesis formation, etc.
5. design science lesson plans based on the **4-E** science learning cycle approach.
6. recognize the advantages and limitations to hands-on science teaching and develop appropriate preparation and classroom management strategies.
7. develop and refine questioning skills necessary to assist children in becoming, creative, critical, and active participants of science.

Assignments upon which your grade will be based include:

1. Successful fulfillment of a **contract** (**10%** of grade) written by you and signed by the Classroom Teacher (due 5th week of the term) which includes:
   a) dates/times of visits
   b) teaching responsibilities
   c) materials or instructional aids to be produced
   d) science topics to be taught
   e) approximate dates for a conference and practicum evaluation.

I realize it may be difficult to be specific for an entire quarter; this should be a guide for your practicum, so don't become overly concerned about specificity, but please do specify the science concepts you believe you will teach.

2. A favorable classroom **teacher evaluation** of your work (**20%** of grade).

3. Team members may elect to submit a group journal provided that each *Daily Reflection* (Part D) is written individually and clearly marked.

Satisfactory completion and submission of your **Field Experience Portfolio,** (**70%** of grade) to include daily log entries which consist of:

A) **an accounting of time** spent teaching and in preparation.

B) **concept map**, two options depending on placement:

After school experience - each week usually consists of a different theme with several activities presented around that one theme. In this setting, choose one of the weekly themes and create a concept map for that theme. Be sure to identify which concepts were covered by the different members of your group at that setting. Each member of that particular field site is encouraged to choose a different week to map.

Traditional classroom experience - you may teach one general topic with several different lessons. In this setting, create a concept map for that theme and identify the concepts you taught. Other teachers may allow you to pick a different topic each week. If so, choose one week and create a concept map for the major heading which your lesson may fall under. Identify the concepts you taught on the map and use linking words to illustrate the connections between and among the concepts.

C) **copies of your lesson plans,**

At least 5 plans must be included accounting for 10 hours of instruction minimum. Your plans must include these factors:

i) 4-E learning cycle format
ii) science process skills for students must be identified
iii) safety precautions must be explained
iv) a complete reference list, including the source for the activity and any useful resources consulted must be included
v) highlight the parts of the plans you were able to complete in the time allotted

D) **daily reflections** on your practicum experience to include:

i) identification and discussion of the **progress** you made toward helping children learn science **concepts** and **process skills**;
ii) descriptions of **methods** you used to teach science;
iii) descriptions of the **science instruction <u>course</u> concepts** that you applied, e.g., questioning, science goals, learning cycle steps, alternative forms of assessment, safety, etc.;
iv) comments about your **successes**; and
v) comments about **improvements** you plan to make.

Concept Map Homework Assignment

Overview: select any science text chapter or from traditional elementary/middle school science teaching materials. Identify the concepts, write concept statements for each concept, map the concepts using the strategies described in Chapter 5 (or those used in the class exercise), and identify the concepts you would choose to teach children or the grade level or age which you specify. Turn the assignment into your instructor for evaluation as a homework assignment. *This assignment may be done as part of a team.*

Specifics:

1. Select any elementary or middle school science text and choose a chapter or similar materials; read it and identify the science concepts.

2. List the science concepts on a sheet of paper. Single words or phrases are sufficient.

3. For the superordinate concept and each coordinating concept, write a succinct statement (sentence) which explains what the concept word means or represents (kind of like a definition of the science to which the concept refers). Refer to class material for good examples and avoid the mistakes of the "non-examples." Please turn in your list of statements with your completed map.

4. Map the concepts; be clear about putting the superordinate concept at the top of your map, coordinating concepts next, and those followed by the subordinate concepts.

5. Draw lines and arrows to illustrate the connections you perceived between and among the concepts and use proposition words to show the conceptual links you wish to reveal.

6. Highlight any concepts you would teach to children (in your lab or otherwise; identify the grade or age level; coordinate with your lab teaching to receive the full benefit of the homework exercise).

7. Submit your work for evaluation by _________________.

Learning Cycle Lesson Plan Template
(3 pages)

Name: ______________ **Lesson Title:** ______________

Grade Level: ______ **Lesson Topic:** ______________

Concepts to be invented: (What is the main science idea? Please state the concept clearly in the form of a complete sentence/definition.)

Additional concepts that are important to Expansion:

Materials Needed:

Safety Precautions and/or Special Procedures:

Phase 1: Exploration (Which process skills will the students use and what will the students do?)

Process skills:

Exploration activity:

Phase 2: Explanation of the Concept (How will you help the students construct the lesson's concept? What key questions will you use and what procedures or steps will be followed?)

Key questions and desired answered:

What procedures/steps will you follow to help students construct the concept? What is the concept state you hope is constructed?

Phase 3: Expansion of the Concept (Which process skills will the students use and what activities will be used? Please explain the procedures or steps to be taken.)

Process Skills:

Activity (procedures/steps):

Please list the principal expansion activities and discussion questions you will use to address any of the following science goals that apply to this lesson.

Science in personal and social perspectives:

Science and technology:

Science as inquiry:

History and nature of science:

Phase 4: Evaluation of the Concept (How will the students show what they have learned? Please list the objectives, outcomes, procedures and/or principal questions you will use to address any of the following:

Hands-On Assessment:

Pictorial Assessment:

Reflective Assessment:

References (What additional references will help support the lesson? Please provide author, title, publisher, date,)

Science Learning Cycle
Lesson Plan Evaluation Form

Name(s): ________________ Course/Date: __________

CRITERIA **RATINGS: Low 1 2 3 4 5 High**

1. *Concept* is clear, succinct and scientifically accurate ________
2. *Safety* precautions identified ________
3. *Exploration* phase is student-centered ________
4. *Exploration* phase instructions do not name/tell the concept ________
5. *Explanation* phase includes a teaching procedure which leads to the concept ________
6. *Explanation* phase introduces/reinforces specific language of the concept ________
7. *Expansion* phase applies the concept ________
8. *Expansion* phase implements national science goals; shows correlation ________
9. *Evaluation* phase contains meaningful behavioral (performance) objectives, outcomes or descriptions which address Hands-On, Pictorial and Reflective Questioning evaluation practices ________
10. *Materials* and/or *references* ________

Average score/grade: ____________

Comments/suggestions:

Science Teaching Evaluation Form

NAME: ______________________ DATE: __________ TOPIC: __________

CRITERIA	RATINGS: Low 1 2 3 4 5 High
Use of Learning Cycle:	
1. Exploration is activity-oriented	______
2. Ample time is given for exploration	______
3. Exploration phase is student-centered with appropriate teacher interaction	______
4. Exploration phase instructions did not name/tell the concept	______
5. Concept is clear and is constructed from the exploration	______
6. Concept phase introduces/reinforces specific vocabulary; is explicit part of lesson	______
7. Expansion has students extend concept to new situations.	______
8. Expansion includes appropriate activities which apply the concept.	______
9. Expansion phase addresses science *goals*	______
About Your Demonstration Lesson:	
10. Clear explanations and directions	______
11. Encourages/Reinforces Pupils	______
12. Questions are appropriate & expand thinking	______
13. Proper questioning skills demonstrated	______
14. Used proper Language Skills	______
15. Effective/efficient materials management	______
16. Proper safety or special procedures	______
17. Enthusiasm, attitude, poise	______
18. Overall effectiveness	______
Total Points/Grade:	______

Comments/Suggestions:

Analysis and Self-Evaluation Paper
Evaluation Form

Name: ____________________ Date: __________

The purpose of this form is to provide succinct feedback and to ensure that all Analysis and Self-Evaluation papers are given equal evaluations by the instructor.

Criteria	**Ratings** **Low** **High** **1 2 3 4 5**
1. Description of the lesson taught	________
2. Summary of video and peer evaluations (quantified, e.g., tables, %ages etc.)	________
3. Description of teaching strengths and weaknesses	________
4. Statement of self-improvement goals	________
5. Quality of writing	________
6. Justified **self-appraisal grade**	________
Grade =	________

Additional Comments:

Field Portfolio Evaluation Form

Name ____________________ Class Section __________

Grading Criteria:

10 = Outstanding; exceeds instructor's expectations
8 - 9 = Very good; shows considerable effort, application, and insight
6 - 7 = Good; journal content item is acceptable
2 - 5 = Needs improvement; item lacks sufficient coverage or description
0 - 1 = Poor; is unacceptable or not included in the journal

Portfolio Contents: **Rating:**

1. **Contract (10 pts)**
   a) dates, times and general responsibilities stated .... ________
   b) science content identified, methods............................ ________

Contract Total ________

2. **Cooperating Teacher Evaluation (20 pts)** .... ________

3. **Portfolio Entries (70 pts)**

   a) Account for time, minimum time fulfilled .... ________

   b) Concept map(s) for the weekly theme or unit taught... ________

   c) Minimum number of lesson plans (5); prefer that one be CD ROM *Science Helper* .... ________

   d) Plans use 4-E Learning Cycle with process skills and safety concerns clearly identified................... ________

   e) Plans address National Science Education Standards science goals .... ________

   f) Daily Reflections show focus on methods and course concepts... ________

   g) Daily entries reflect on weaknesses, successes, and suggest improvements................... ________

Total of Portfolio Entries: ______

FIELD EXPERIENCE GRADE = ______

Comments:

Chapter 1 Outline

WHAT IS SCIENCE?

Overview T1.0

This chapter reports a summary of childrens' common perceptions about science and scientists, and brief comparisons of science performances. Considerable improvement has been made during the past 10 years. However, achievement scores show that U.S. children generally understand science facts well, but that they can not use what they know to analyze and problem solve. Some underlying reasons for this discrepancy may be linked to how science is viewed and taught by teachers. The chapter makes a case that science, when taught wholistically, produces an effective synergy that arises from including three important parts of science: attitudes, processes and knowledge. Any one part emphasized at the expense of the other two leaves children's science learning incomplete, hence affecting academic performance. Science is a dynamic human enterprise; it is not static. The aim of modern science is to promote scientific literacy for all children, not a select few. New National Science Education Standards seek this aim holistically through systemic reform with a focus on quality science experiences, rather than on quantity. Quality may be accomplished by covering less, but learning more, including all of science's parts. The chapter concept map tells the story of the chapter; you may wish to copy and distribute it to your students.

Outline

I. What Are Childrens' Perceptions of Science?

T1.1 A. Science is ...

T1.2 B. Scientists are ...

II. Where Is Elementary and Middle School Science?

T1.3 A. International comparisons

1. US elementary children rank 9 of 12
2. US secondary students rank much lower

T1.4 B. Present Indicators

1. average classroom time per day increased
2. early exposure to science benefits children
3. number of women receiving science degrees increased
4. proficiency scores increased overall (T1.5)

T1.6 C. U.S. comparisons

1. science proficiency has increased for all ages during the past decade
2. high scores on understanding science facts
3. low scores on using science content
4. white urban students score higher than minority, disadvantaged youth
5. young children like science, even though half of schools do not treat it as a priority

T1.7, T1.8 6. the number of minutes per day spent teaching science has increased for grades 1-6 during the past decade

II. The Nature of Science

T1.9 A. Philosophy and perception shapes what science is

T1.10 B. Attitudes influence readiness, are learned, and direct learner experiences

1. emotional attitudes, like curiosity, are fundamental
2. intellectual attitudes, like skepticism and tolerance, encourage objectivity and skills

C. Process skills enable children to learn and to problem-solve

T1.11 1. basic process skills, like observing, classifying, and communicating, are essential for all ages

T1.12 2. integrated process skills, like controlling variables, hypothesizing, and graphing, are appropriate for intermediate grades and above and are essential if children are to experiment and solve problems

T1.13 D. Science knowledge (e.g., facts and concepts) are the outcomes of attitudinally motivated process skills

III. Whole Science

T1.14 A. Includes a healthy blend of experiences that nurture attitudes, processes and knowledge

B. Is greater than the sum of its individual parts

C. Is a natural way for children to learn

IV. Aims of Modern Science

A. Scientific literacy for all (p. 27 definition from *Benchmarks*)

B. Standards based on "covering less, but doing more" philosophy

T1.15 C. Accomplished by a whole science approach

Chapter 2 Outline

HOW DO CHILDREN LEARN SCIENCE?

Overview   T2.0

This chapter describes the relationships among children ideas and needs, dominant theoretical perspectives on how they learn, and the ways in which teachers' perspectives of their own roles influence children's learning. Children bring preconceptions to their classes. Misconceptions may have been formed from prior experiences. The ideas that children already possess impact on what and how they learn science. As well, children have similar needs, overall, but vary in extent of development. A synthesis of contemporary perspectives on learning is used to describe constructivism, the present most comprehensive explanation for how we believe children learn science. The need for direct, hands-on, minds-on experiences with special attention to concept formation and the development of science mental structures shapes our view of what teaching practices and types of teachers are essential for effective learning in science.

Outline

T2.1 I. How Do Children's Ideas Influence Their Learning?

T2.2 A. Preconceptions are often incomplete attempts at explaining the natural world

T2.3 B. Misconceptions are alternative understandings that are scientifically incorrect

T2.4 II. What Do We Know About Children's Ideas?

A. Prior ideas are personal, arise from perceptions, linked to experience

B. Prior ideas are contradictory, child perceives no need for consistency

C. Prior ideas resist change, difficult to correct misconceptions

T2.5 II. What Do Children Need To Help Them Learn?

A. Thinking requires multisensory stimulation

B. Physical activity provides experiences essential for thinking and language development

C. Language development arises from rich experiences

D. Socialization develops over time and is related to academic achievement

E. Self-esteem is nurtured through cooperation rather than competition

F. Time is needed for individual development and cannot be accelerated

T2.6 III. What Is The Dominant Perspective On Science Learning?

T2.7 A. Constructivism assumes knowledge cannot exist outside the mind of the learner

T2.8 B. Constructivist continuum; illustrates different degrees of the theory

T2.9 C. Constructivist teachers strive to create meaningful learning opportunities

T2.10 D. Jean Piaget

1\. cognitive development theory sheds light on how mental structures may be formed

2\. progressive and overlapping stage development

T2.11 3. theoretical concept of equilibrium maintenance is key

T2.12, 2.13 4. concepts of assimilation and accommodation describe the process of equilibrium and formation of cognitive structures

E. Constructivism

T2.14 1. uses learner's prior ideas to build concepts, correct misconceptions, and develop mental conceptual structures

2\. relies on hands-on minds learning

T2.15 4. encourages variety of learning strategies

T2.16 5. 4-E teaching and learning model satisfies student learning needs: explore, explain, expand, evaluate

Chapter 3 Outline

HOW CAN YOU TEACH SCIENCE FOR ALL CHILDREN?

Overview T3.0

Typically when we think of children who are exceptional, we may consider children who are gifted and talented or who have disabilities. Actually the range is much greater. In this chapter we assume the posture that all children will benefit from the many techniques used to assist those who are classified as exceptional. We make a case that each child is unique and we strive to help readers learn how to overcome stereotypes. This chapter includes coverage of multicultural education issues, language differences, gender differences, learning style differences, learning disabilities, mental disabilities, physical disabilities, and giftedness. A unique aspect of this chapter is the section that gives ideas for working with parents to teach children science.

Content

T3.1 I. Science For All
- A. Multicultural education
  1. all children are different

  T3.2 2. multiple cultures include race, religion, economic level, ethnicity, language differences, and gender

  T3.3 3. NSTA position statement
     - a. access for all
     - b. select and use materials that incorporate diversity
     - c. identify learning style preferences
     - d. expose to career opportunities
  4. use differences to promote greater understanding
     - a. use science themes
     - b. select teaching examples that show diversity
     - c. consider myths, dispel
     - d. challenge inaccurate statements
     - e. develop special provisions for those who need them
  5. characteristics to observe
     - a. different experiences
     - b. action rather than words
     - c. limited vocabulary
     - d. disorganization
     - e. need for nourishing relationships
     - f. feelings of hopelessness and desperation

T3.4 B. Non-English-Speaking students
  1. help students help themselves
     - a. vocabulary lists and study aids

        b. pocket references
        c. invite questions
        d. use patience
        e. encourage written translations
        f. encourage reading in own language
    2. hear: forget, see: remember, do: understand
    3. reduce test anxiety
        a. puzzles
        b. drawings
        c. self-check work
        d. bonus points and extra credit

T3.5 C. Gender equality
    1. unequal access for females, sex role stereotypes
    2. cultural disincentives and insufficient background
    3. teacher influence on sex-role stereotypes
T3.6 4. model for overcoming stereotypes
        a. different expectations are formed
        b. believe females are as capable as males
        c. encourage females to lead
        d. maintain equal contact with males and females
        e. provide opportunities for success
    5. overcome gender inequality
        a. strengthen science preparation
        b. become aware of own biases
        c. try single-sex groups
        d. expect same from females as from males
        e. be aware of barriers against females
        f. promote hand-on learning for all
        g. present gender-free science
        h. screen teaching materials for gender bias
        i. include female science role models
T3.7 6. bringing gender equity to science lessons
        a. connect science and technology to the real world
        b. choose appropriate metaphors
        c. foster collaboration
        d. encourage females to be experts
        e. have females control technology
        f. portray technology as a way to solve problems
        g. capitalize with females verbal strengths
        h. experiment with testing and evaluation
        i. keep expectations high
        j. experiment with techniques

D. Similarities in learning
    1. "learning styles" are the ways we prefer to process information as we learn
T3.8 2. types of learning styles
        a. visual
        b. auditory
        c. kinesthetic

d. individual
e. group
f. verbal
g. written
h. sequential
i. global
j. interactions of the above

T3.9,3.10 3. teaching suggestions
a. routines
b. limited choices
c. attending to instructions and material
d. memory clues
e. sequence
f. separate testing from instruction
g. specific praise and criticism
h. time clues
i. confer with special education and gifted teachers
j. show empathy, encouragement, sensitivity
k. hands-on learning opportunities
l. set clear expectations
m. give frequent feedback
n. start with learner's preferred learning mode

T3.11 II. Science For Exceptional Children (see Table 3.1)

A. Learning disabilities
1. oral expression
2. listening comprehension
3. written expression
4. basic reading skills
5. reading comprehension
6. mathematical calculations
7. mathematical reasoning

B. Intellectual handicaps
1. educable mentally retarded capable of learning

T3.12 2. use concept analysis strategy for planning and teaching (Fig 3.2)

C. Physical disabilities
1. visual
2. hearing
3. orthopedic
4. use strategies that stimulate non-impaired senses and that overcome orthopedic limitations

D. Gifted and talented learners
1. capable of superior progress
2. use open-ended learning activities
3. use as classroom teaching resources
4. reinforce and rewards superior effort and success

T3.13 III. How Can Parents Help Meet Children's Special Needs?

A. Inform about the importance of science to careers and future success
B. Parents help children study and prepare
C. Make extra home science activities available

Chapter 4 Outline

WHAT GOALS PROMOTE SCIENTIFIC LITERACY?

<u>Overview</u> T4.0

Science permeates every aspect of our lives, as well as those of young children. Knowing about science and being able to use it for its personal, professional, social, technological and/or social benefits requires that science be considered a basic among school subject and skill areas. Indeed, this modern view of science implies a revised definition of scientific literacy that requires new goals for school science programs. The recent reform efforts in science consider what children need to help them succeed in a world that has become more socially and technologically complex. While these science goals may be described differently by the organizations that propose reform, their central intentions seem to be to help children understand, use, and appreciate science in ways that support the concept of whole science (previously described in Chapter 1). The chapter presents several "new dimensions" drawn from the National Science Education Standards for program content.

<u>Outline</u>

T4.1 I. What Is Scientific Literacy?
- A. National Research Council's definition includes
  1. attitudes necessary for "research"
  2. ability to discern, comprehend, and communicate
  3. capability to identify relevant issues, and form and express a position
  4. ability to evaluate information based on evidence
- B. Literacy evolves and is developed over a life time
- T4.2, 4.3 C. Positive "scientific" attitudes elevate achievement and self-esteem
- T4.4, 4.5 D. Science process skills are literacy tools vital to adult living

II. What Reform Efforts have Sought To Provide Goals For Scientific Literacy?
- T4.6, 4.7 A. *Project Synthesis,* 4 outcomes illustrate an era of new goals
- T4.8 B. *Scope, Sequence, and Coordination of Secondary School Science,* eliminates "layer cake" approach to science curricula
- T4.9 C. *Project 2061,* 10 principles influence new goals, organized around themes
- T4.10,4.11 D. *National Science Education Standards*, nation-wide and system-wide effort to reform science education
  1. teaching standards
  2. professional teacher development standards
  3. assessment in science education standards
  4. science content standards
  5. science education program standards
  6. science education system standards

T4.12 III. Goals To Promote Scientific Literacy

T4.13 A. 4 New Dimensions of Science Content Outcomes

T4.14 B. Dimension 1: Science as Inquiry

T4.15 C. Dimension 2: Science and Technology

T4.16 D. Dimension 3: Science in Personal and Social Perspectives

T4.17 E. Dimension 4: History and Nature of Science

Chapter 5 Outline

PLANNING: HOW CAN YOU PLAN EFFECTIVE SCIENCE INSTRUCTION?

Overview T 5.0

"If it isn't planned, it isn't likely to happen." is one principle of effective teaching that guides this chapter. A teacher who does not get beyond doing the "gee-wow" part of an activity and spend time guiding students as they construct the reason why the activity is important, may actually help feed student misconceptions. The chapter emphasizes planning for concept formation. Concept mapping techniques are explained and illustrated. A useful mapping activity could be to use school science texts, have methods students identify science concepts in a chapter, write concepts on cards, and sort the cards into a structure or hierarchy as a way to learn about the techniques of concept mapping (see Concept Mapping video supplied with the instructor's manual and refer to course suggestions in the first section of this manual). Mapping can help teachers clarify goals, set realistic outcomes and objectives, and develop useful lessons. The chapter illustrates how a constructivist teaching method can be used to help students form concepts as they advance toward the goals of modern science. This example plan illustrates the form we have used for all of the lessons in our book; the plan and teaching approach address each new dimension of the NSES content goals. Evaluation should be considered as a part of planning. Therefore, this chapter devotes substantial space and attention to the tools of hands-on, pictorial and reflection questioning assessments, as well as uses of portfolios and rubrics. Several useful evaluation techniques are also illustrated in the chapter.

Outline

T5.1,5.2 I. Concept Mapping

T5.3 A. Concept maps

1. make abstractions more concrete
2. shows relationships among concepts
3. develops a hierarchy
4. helps children connect new and old ideas
5. helps children construct meaningful patterns
6. helps children avoid and reverse misconceptions
7. can be used as lesson organizers
8. can be used as a form of student evaluation

T5.4,5.5 B. Parts of concept maps

1. superordinate concept: the main concept at the top of a map
2. coordinating concepts: the first row of concepts
3. subordinate concept: all other concepts
4. propositions: linking words that describe the relationship between concepts
5. facts: single ideas that do not have predictive value

T5.6,5.7 D. Steps for constructing concept maps
1. identify and list all concepts in a lesson, chapter, etc.
2. isolate specific facts
3. select the superordinate concept
4. arrange subordinate concepts beginning with the coordinating concepts
5. draw lines to illustrate relationships between concepts
6. write propositions to make relationships clear
7. identify specific concepts to be emphasized in a lesson
8. use map to plan the steps of a lesson

II. Planning Constructivist Science Lessons

T5.8 A. Selecting or developing unit activities
1. provide a variety of activities for learning.
2. use special vocabulary and introduce concept after children have first hand experiences
3. interact with children and with each other
4. focus experiences so children can construct concepts
5. help student make connections between concepts

T5.9 B. Developing Objectives
1. emphasize the student and identify what students should do
2. four parts: A, B, C, D
3. emphasis on observation or measurement of pupil performance
4. include science attitudes and processes in objectives

III. Planning the Lesson

A. 4-E approach recommended (Fig 5.5, Exhibit 5.1)
1. nurtures pupil construction of knowledge
2. promotes concept formation

T5.10 B. Exploration provides essential experiences

T5.11 C. Explanation helps learners to construct the lesson's concept

T5.12 D. Expansion helps students to organize thinking, form concept structures, and benefit from science goals

T5.13,14,15 E. Evaluation is a part of instruction and determines extent to which objectives have been accomplished, see Table 5.1

T5.16,17 IV. How Can You Evaluate Student Learning?

T5.18 A. Limits and purposes of tests, see Table 5.1

B. Selecting the tool for the task, see Table 5.1

T5.19 C. Pictorial assessment, see Fig. 5.6, 5.7

T5.20 D. Reflective questioning, see Fig. 5.8, 5.9

T5.21 E. Hands-on assessment, see Fig. 5.10. 5.11, 5.12

F. Teacher records and observations, see Fig. 5.13, 5.14

T5.22 G. Rubrics, see Fig. 5.15, 5.16

T5.23 H. Systematic Observation, see Fig. 5.17, 5. 18 ,Tables 5.2, 5.3

T5.24 I. Student self-assessments

Supplemental Lesson

The following lesson extends the learner experiences and the concepts. You might want to consider combining Exhibit 5.1 (the example in the chapter) with the additional lesson shown below.

Lesson Topic: Electricity - Filaments Role in a Bulb

Grade Level: 6 - 8 **Discipline:** Physical Science

Concepts to be invented: main idea - -The wires in a bulb (the filament) make it part of a complete circuit and provide enough resistance to cause the filament to glow.

Additional concepts that are important to expansion: filament, circuit, Nichrome wire, resistance.

Materials Needed:

D-cell batteries, battery holders and clips, flashlight size bulbs, a lamp bulb with frosted glass covering removed or a clear glass light bulb, bulb holders, plasticene, copper wire #20, Nichrome wire #32, wire cutters.

Safety Precautions:

The students should be reminded to use caution around the bulb in which the glass has been removed. When creating their own bulb they should NOT touch the exposed wires.

1. **Exploration:** ***Which process skills will be used?***
Hypothesizing, inferring, formulating models, recording data, observing
What will the children do?
Instructions: Give your students the following challenge: "Without looking at a bulb, try to draw one. Be as detailed as possible about what is going on in the inside. Use your previous knowledge about circuits to assist you in your task." Once they have completed their drawings have the students obtain a flashlight bulb and compare their drawing to it. Using the copper wires, battery and bulb, complete a circuit. Could you have completed the circuit with a bulb like the one you drew?

2. **Explanation = Concept Invention:** ***What is the main idea? How will the main idea be identified?***

Concept: The wires in a bulb (the filament) make it part of a complete circuit.

Allow the students to examine a lamp light bulb with the frosted glass removed. While they are doing this ask them the following: Where does the electricity go inside the bulb? Why do you think this? Where do you think the wires go inside the base of the bulb? Why? What happens when one wire touches the case and the other wire touches the tip? What makes the bulb light?

The electricity goes up into the bulb and through the wire which we call a *filament*. This filament is the part from which the light comes. One wire goes to the base tip and one goes to the metal case because you had to touch both the case and the tip to make the bulb light. When the wire touches the case and the light bulb it is a closed circuit, or continuous circle, and the light comes on. The filament is not a good conductor of electricity (it provides resistance, another useful concept to study), much of the energy gets turned into heat, and the heat makes the light glow.

3. Expansion of the Idea: *Which process skills will be used?*

Inferring, observing, predicting, designing an experiment, manipulating materials, recording and analyzing data.

How will the idea be expanded?

Provide the students with the following materials: A strip of plasticene, two battery assemblies (battery, holder, clips), three 15 cm. pieces of bare copper wire, one 5 cm. piece of #32 (thin) Nichrome wire, and wire cutters.

Ask the students to look at the pictures they drew of a bulb that worked correctly and then to design a way they could use the materials provided to make their own bulb. Caution them not to touch the wires once they have completed their circuit. Ask them to plan with a peer possible arrangements of the materials. Record the method you designed. Now try it out. Did it work? If it didn't, what might you change to get it to work? Try again.

Additional Concept Invention: *How will the concept be identified?*

Concept: a thinner wire provides more resistance than a thicker wire of the same material.

What happens when the circuit is closed? Why do you think it glows? How is the Nichrome wire in your bulb the same as the filament in a regular household light bulb? Different? The nichrome wire glows when the circuit is closed. The Nichrome wire has more resistance than the copper wire therefore the wire heats up and glows. The Nichrome wire is similar to a regular household light bulb since it glows and gives off light, but it doesn't last as long. There must be another factor that makes the company made bulbs last longer. There is a gas in them and that is why the bulbs pop when they break. Some gases that might be inside are nitrogen or argon.

Science in Personal and Social Perspectives

1. What do you think might be a possible cause for the light bulbs in your home to burn out?
2. What could be a possible explanation for the following dilemma: You replaced a burned out bulb with what you thought was a new one, and the bulb would not light?

Science and Technology

1. Where else might this idea of using a thin wire such as a filament in a circuit be utilized? How has the application of this concept assisted in the manufacturing of things like toasters? Houses?
2. How has the invention of the light bulb changed the quality of life for people throughout the world?

Science as Inquiry

1. Expansion concepts include: resistance, resistance in relation to wire size, resistance in relation to type of conducting material.
2. New concepts to be identified for invention in new lessons: fuses, flow of electrons, changing electric to heat energy.
3. Working knowledge of circuit, filament, resistance in relation to thin or thick wire.

History and Nature of Science

1. Thomas Edison tried many materials in order to come up with the perfect filament for his light bulb. If you were working with him today, what advice or assistance could you offer him?
2. In 1912, Thomas Edison was to share the Nobel prize in physics with Nikola Tesla. What did these two men have in common and why did they never receive the prize? [Edison felt direct current , DC, was the best way to transmit electricity over wires. The Croation-American electrical engineer, Nikola Tesla (1856-1943) developed transformers which work with alternating current, AC. Tesla believed this was a much more efficient means of transporting electricity. Tesla refused to be associated with Edison, therefore the Nobel prize committee awarded the prize to a Swedish inventor instead.]

4. Evaluation: *How will the students show what they have learned?*

Upon completing the activities the students will be able to:

- correctly identify the base, base contact, lead-in wires, filament and bulb when given a diagram like the one below.

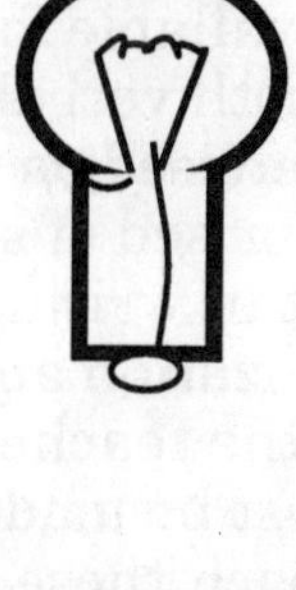

- determine what other materials are needed in order to design a way to determine which of these wires has greater resistance, when given three different gauges of wire. The child will then be able to carry out his/her design plans.

- determine why the bulb is not lighting, when given what appears to be a closed circuit.

Chapter 6

HOW CAN YOU CREATE A SAFE, EFFICIENT, ACTIVITY-BASED SCIENCE CLASSROOM?

Overview T6.0

This chapter merges two important functions: classroom space and materials management, and safe science. We begin with safety, believing that one who develops an attitude of thinking safely also plans and functions for safe and efficient learning. Each supports enjoyable constructivist experiences for learners and teachers. The reader is asked two key questions that should guide them in planning any activities related to the science classroom: 1) What is the educational value of the activity? 2) What are the foreseeable hazards associated with the activity? A detailed discussion of the legal responsibilities for the classroom teacher and various safety factors about matters such as field trips, chemical storage, classroom space and maintenance, and equipment use and maintenance are included in this chapter. Excerpts from the *Total Science Safety System* are included in the chapter. Readers are invited to examine the safety forms and files found on this customizable computer disk. Materials include: Life, Earth, and Physical science activities and procedures, a sample student safety contract, an accident/incident report form, and a sample request form for correction of safety problems.

In planning any science activity the safety concerns should be addressed before the activity begins. Would other teachers with similar training attempt to do this activity? Is it appropriate for the physical and mental development levels of my students? Do I have adequate safety equipment available for my students? Safety equipment concerns should be pointed out both verbally and in writing to school administrators. Due care should be exercised as the students are engaged in the activity. Students should be apprised of safety rules before any activities begin, and students should assist in writing safety contracts. Safe science questions such as these lead to organization and management of the classroom and materials.

Once the teacher knows the science concepts to be taught then decisions must be made as to what kinds of materials will be necessary to effectively teach those concepts. Tips on what and how to order materials are provided in this chapter. A discussion of classroom storage versus central storage is included. Key to the storage question is how the classroom will be managed. Will the classroom atmosphere be one where science exploration can go on freely? Will the students be allowed access to science materials for individual exploration or will materials only be made available at certain times of the day? Will science teaching take place in large or small groups? Will a science learning center be maintained? This chapter also provides the future teacher with a form to assist in planning science activities, a list and description of commonly used supplies, science equipment checkout form, floor plans and design ideas for arranging an activity based science classroom.

Outline

T6.1 I. What Are Your Legal Responsibilities?
T6.2 A. Legal definition

1. Tort
2. Reasonable and Prudent Judgment
3. Foreseeability (Figure 6.1)

T6.3 4. Negligence

5. Due Care
    a. instruction
        i. rules should be clearly defined
        ii. students should sign a safety contract
        iii. teachers should be role models for safety (Fig. 6.2)

T6.4 b. supervision
        i. overcrowded classrooms are cause for many accidents (Fig. 6.3)
        ii. class size should be limited to 24
        iii. field trips need consent forms and proper supervision (fig. 6.4)

B. Federal and State Legislation

T6.5 1. Eye protective equipment standards

2. Types and uses of goggles

II. Safety Equipment

T6.6 A. Electrical

B. Heating materials

T6.7 C. Flammable liquid storage

D. Loose clothing and long hair

E. Fire blankets

T6.8 F. Fire extinguishers

G. Eyewash and shower

T6.9 III. Performing Safety Assessments

A. Classrooms and Field Trips

B. Science safety checklist (Fig. 6.5)

C. *Total Science Safety System*

IV. What Materials Are Necessary For The Activities?

T6.10 A. Necessary Materials

1. items purchased through a scientific supplier

T6.11 (Figs 6.6, 6.7, 6.9

2. items purchased locally

3. items made from recycled materials

T6.12&13V. Storage

A. Central

B. Classroom

T6.14 C. Storing and dispensing materials

T6.15 VI. Room Arrangement (Fig. 6.11)

A. Large group science activities

T6.16 B. Science learning centers (Figs. 6.12, 6.13, Table 6.2)

C. Bulletin boards/ displays

Chapter 7 Outline

WHAT ARE THE CHARACTERISTICS OF EFFECTIVE SCIENCE MATERIALS AND PROGRAMS?

<u>Overview</u> T7.0

As with that reference to history -- those who are unfamiliar with the mistakes of the past are doomed to repeat them -- this chapter examines examples of past effective science programs. The historical precedents set by past science programs helped to shape the present criteria we use the identify effective programs. Those same criteria may be used for screening the multitude of science materials available. The future is described in terms of innovative programs now available, but which may be regarded at "futuristic" by many schools for whom constructivist science is a new concept. Three key programs are compared in the historical portion of this chapter. These program are available and used by schools. Their contrasts and similarities help to lay a foundation for the excellence criteria that is given in the "What Research Says" section of the chapter. These criteria come from the National Science Teachers Association and are exemplified by the many examples of the next generation of science programs that are described in brief. These programs are further examples of the uses of science resources, which is the subject of Chapter 8, and which you may wish to correlate with this chapter.

<u>Outline</u>

T7.1 I. Dominant Beliefs in Science Education
- A. Quality and excellence are two goals
- B. Conflicting beliefs about what science is and about what is quality science education
- C. Conflicts reveal the deeper issues surrounding quality and excellence

II. Changes Over Time: Legacy Of The Past
- A. Fields are no longer distinct
- B. Hybrid specialization and knowledge explosion blurs lines between fields
- C. Pupil conformity and getting back to the basics are misguided goals

III. Major Elementary Science Program Models: Looking Back For The Source Of Wisdom

T7.2 A. Alphabet Soup (Table 7.1)
1. decade after Sputnik (1957) spawned many models

T7.3 2. experimental model programs supported by similar needs and goals, but proceed with different methods (Fig 7.1: SAPA, SCIS, ESS)

T7.4 B. SAPA: Science - A Process Approach

1. highly structured, applies behavioral psychology
2. emphasizes development of process skills: basic and integrated (Fig 7.2,7.3)
3. approach stimulated greatest gain in processes (Table 7.2)
4. also improved student science attitudes and achievement

T7.5 C. SCIS: Science Curriculum Improvement Study

1. moderate structure; emphasizes science concepts (Fig 7.4)
2. learning cycle developed; basis for much of today's constructivist science teaching
3. stimulated greatest gains in science achievement
4. stimulated gains in process skills, creativity, and other study skill areas

T7.6 D. ESS: Elementary Science Study

1. flexible organization, promotes personal discovery
2. content units organized around interesting themes or unit topics (Fig. 7.6)
3. stimulated greatest gains in pupil attitudes toward science
4. positive gains in achievement, process skills, creativity

T7.7 IV. What Works?

A. Direct instruction

1. majority of all science classes use a textbook exclusively
2. preference for or belief that direct instruction is most effective

T7.8 B. Hands-on, minds-on instruction (Table 7.2)

1. produces significant gains in achievement, processes, attitudes and other skills
2. pronounced benefits for disadvantaged students
3. thinking improves
4. provides more intrinsic rewards for learners
5. greater transfer of learning
6. learner retention improves

C. Criteria for excellence (see What Research Says)

1. demonstrate student growth
2. hands-on, minds-on instruction through practical experiences
3. instruction receives adequate support and integrates other subjects into science
4. teachers must understand and use modern science goals, experiment with approaches, provide varied learning experiences, and use technology in effective ways

T7.9 D. Supported assumptions

1. effective programs are cutting edge with vision and professionally active teachers
2. effective programs have a conceptual focus and use student-centered teaching methods
3. effective programs select content carefully and make it useful for all learners
4. effective programs attempt to cover less material, but have children do more with the selected topics

T7.10 V. The Next Generation

A. New programs developed from what works -- lessons learned from past experiments
B. New programs promote multiple teaching methods and interesting materials to fill multiple student needs and interests
C. New programs use organizing themes to focus concepts (Table 7.3)
D. Nine example programs described; more in Chapter 8 and appendix

Chapter 8

HOW CAN YOU IMPROVE YOUR SCIENCE INSTRUCTION THROUGH HUMAN, PRINT, AND MULTIMEDIA RESOURCES?

Overview T8.0

Reasons are discussed in Chapter 12 for the importance of using additional resources (other than the science textbook) and the identification of those additional resources. While the use of additional resources requires time and planning, they are the key to enhancing instruction. Resources assist in making learning personal, they enhance student interest and increase learning opportunities. Resources help make the link between the community and the classroom, the link between science and society, between societal and ethical concerns, and the link between emerging technologies and the dissemination of career information.

Resources come in many forms. First and foremost are the human resources. These may be your colleagues - other teachers, upper grade level students, or community members. Professional organizations such as the National Science Teachers Association, the state department of education, or places like NASA and even 4H can be useful resources for a science teacher. Other types of resources may come in the form of telecommunication networks, alliances or partnerships with businesses, field trips, or educational television programs. This chapter provides tips to get resource people involved with the classroom, ways to work with volunteers in the schools, a list of science concepts and related careers, the benefits of an alliance, and describes the quality indicators to look for when screening multimedia materials.

Outline

T8.1 I. Why Use Supplemental Resources?
- A. Enhance instruction; strengthen the curriculum
- B. Increase student interest; strengthen skills
- C. Create links between science concepts, society, and technology, and illuminate the rich history of science

II. What Are the Resources Available?

T8.2 A. Human Resources
- 1. Colleagues
- 2. Volunteers (see Tables 8.1, 8.2)

T8.3 B. Organizational and Agency Supports (see Appendices C,D,E)
- 1. Professional Organizations
  - a. National Science Teachers Association is the leading profession group for science educators
  - b. Many state have local affiliates for NSTA with separate conferences
- 2. State and Federal Agencies

a. U.S. Department of Agriculture provide services for K-12 and 4H activities
b. The National Aeronautics and Space Administration (NASA) has regional centers with teacher resource rooms available
3. State Departments of Education

T8.4 C. Telecommunication Networks
1. make use of computer links across computer highways
T8.5 2. increase professionalism among teachers, facilitate communication
3. Is the material worthwhile? (Table 8.3)

Chapter 9 Outline

WHAT TEACHING METHODS HELP LEARNERS TO CONSTRUCT MEANING?

Overview T9.0

Distinctions are made between inquiry and discovery. Processes of inquiry, which are consistent with the National Science Education Standards, are described and demonstrated through the teaching methods described in the chapter. All methods encourage children to discover and to form science concepts, to construct their understanding. The methods included in the chapter include: science learning cycle, scientific method as a teaching method, Suchman's inquiry, and children learning science through play. Tips for turning children's questions into a method of inquiry and recommendations for successful inquiry teaching are explained. Management tips are described for using cooperative learning strategies in science.

Content

T9.1 I. What are Inquiry and Discovery?
- A. Inquiry is a process for finding out
- B. Discovery is what is found, the learner's mental construction

II. Constructivist Science Teaching Methods
- T9.2 A. The science learning cycle (see Exhibit 9.1 for an example)
  - T9.3 1. a method for planning lessons and for teaching that is consistent with how children construct understanding (Fig 9.1, 9.2)
  - T9.4 2. phase 1: Exploration is learner-centered, stimulates disequilibrium, and encourages mental assimilation
  - T9.5 3. phase 2: Explanation is more teacher-centered, focuses on concept formation and nurtures learner mental accommodation
  - T9.6 4. phase 3: Expansion becomes more student-centered and encourages group cooperation as well as deeper mental concept structures
  - T9.7, 9.8 5. phase 4: Evaluation may be integrated into any step and seeks to determine if proper conception has developed
- T9.9 B. The scientific method as a teaching method (Fig 9.3)
  1. step 1: students conclude that an experiment will provide the best answer to the science question or dilemma
  2. step 2: focus the question to seek a specific science answer
  3. step 3: guess an answer and use references to find out if

the answer is already known
4. step 4: use guiding questions to find out the answer to the question in step 2
5. step 5: have students apply what they learn from experimentation; after they form a conclusion, use it in a practical way

T9.10 C. Suchman's inquiry
T9.11 1. based on use of discrepant events (Fig 9.4, 9.5)
T9.12 2. step 1: present the discrepant event
3. step 2: have students ask yes/no questions to verify the events and to collect new information
4. step 3: encourage student discussion of what is known and to research in library further, if needed
5. step 4: discuss to construct the best explanation for the discrepancy

D. Can children learn science through play? (Fig 9.6)
1. based on the theories of Dewey and Piaget in the spirit of constructivism
2. stage 1: children do experiment teacher has proposed
3. step 2: children repeat the experiment with variation to expand experiences
4. stage 3: elaborate on experiences
5. stage 4: children initiate own "experiments"
6. stage 5: communicate with parents about their child's interest
7. stage 6: new experiments proposed by teacher

T9.13 E. Children's questions as inquiry teaching methods (Table 9.1)
T9.14 1. step 1: invite and record children's questions
2. step 2: decide which questions to investigate
3. step 3: help children plan investigations (Table 9.2)
4. step 4: monitor investigations and assist
5. step 5: help children record and report what they find

T9.15 F. Cooperative inquiry groups (Table 9.3)
1. <u>principal investigator</u> manages the group and checks the assignment
2. <u>materials manager</u> collects and distributes all equipment
3. <u>recorder</u> collects and records all pertinent information that represents the group's investigation
4. <u>reporter</u> communicates the results, verbally or in writing, to the teacher or class
5. <u>maintenance director</u> is in <u>charge</u> of cleanup, is not solely responsible for doing the cleanup

T9.16 III. Successful inquiry teachers (Table 9.4):

A. Model scientific attitudes
B. Are creative
C. Are flexible
D. Use effective questioning strategies
E. Focus their efforts on preparing children to think

Chapter 10 Outline

WHAT DO YOU NEED TO KNOW ABOUT USING QUESTIONS AS A SCIENCE TEACHING TOOL?

Overview   T10.0

Questions are essential tools necessary for stimulating science inquiry processes, which lead to student concept construction. In science, skillful questioning is useful for planning, leading lessons, stimulating productive thinking, and for assuring that children's science discoveries that are constructed from direct experiences that are conceptually accurate. Talented and conscientious teachers can use their questioning skills to create or to customize teaching methods. This utility value of questions and questioning processes, along with the multiple other uses of questions, qualifies questioning as a fundamental and universal teaching tool. This chapter poses, in pre-test fashion, several important questions about the uses of questions in science teaching, and the effects of questions on children's science achievement, attitudes and thinking skills. The chapter also explores the different types of questions and helps readers to investigate how questions may be used to teach science. Suggestions are offered to help teachers to develop their questioning skills, monitor their uses, and to improve their own questions. A unique aspect of the chapter is the section that deals with using children's questions. The applications of this chapter are continued in the other chapters on teaching methods.

Outline

T10.1,10.2   I. Questions on Questions (Fig 10.1)

T10.3   A. What kinds of questions do teachers ask and what kinds of answers do they require?
1. low level
2. factual answers

T10.4   B. Why do teachers use questions? (Table 10.1)
1. to evaluate
2. to control
3. to instruct

T10.5   C. How do questions affect students?
1. questions shape attitudes, thinking and achievement
2. questions can stimulate high level and divergent thinking
3. higher level questions with wait-time, redirection and probing stimulate improved achievement

T10.6   D. How are teacher questions and student answers related?
1. positive relations between level of question and level of answer
2. positive effect on language development of young children

T10.7 E. How do teachers use questions to involve all students? (Fig 10.2)

1. helps to adapt instruction to student diversity
2. can be used to encourage greater involvement of low achievers
3. can be used to initiate contact for providing essential feedback

T10.8 F. What is "wait-time" and why is it important (Fig 10.3, 10.4)

1. wait-time is the length of time one waits after asking a question before rephrasing or redirecting the question, or probing or reinforcing the response
2. average wait-time is less than 1 second
3. recommend extension of wait-time to 3-5 seconds
4. advantages include improvements in the quality and quantity of student participation, with improved confidence and cooperation

T10.9 G. What types of questions are used most in elementary science books and tests?

1. majority are low level questions devoted to facts
2. about 95% of test questions are devoted to Bloom's Knowledge and Comprehension levels
3. teacher should screen texts, tests, and other print materials re: questions and adapt as necessary

T10.10 II. What are the Different Types of Questions?

A. Good Questions

1. stimulate and invite the child to explore and guide toward an answer
2. refer to children's experiences, real objects or events
3. invite children to demonstrate an answer
4. science process skills questions invite the qualities listed above (see *What Research Says* and Exercise 10.1)

B. Bloom's Taxonomy (Fig 10.5)

1. knowledge - remember facts
2. comprehension - express in own words
3. application - use information in a new context
4. analysis - break down into parts
5. synthesis - develop original ideas or solutions
6. evaluation - make choices and defend

T10.11 C. Gallagher and Aschner (see Table 10.2, Fig 10.6, Exercise 10.2)

1. cognitive memory - recall facts and information, similar to Bloom's knowledge and comprehension levels
2. convergent - apply and analyze
3. divergent - stimulate independent thought
4. evaluative - choose, judge and defend or criticize

T10.12 III. What are the Keys to Effective Questioning?

A. Plan specific questions
B. Ask simply, concisely and directly
C. Ask before selecting respondent
D. Use wait-time
E. Listen to responses for proper level
F. Question to produce conceptual conflict (Piaget cognitive dissonance is an example)

T10.13

G. Talk less and ask more
H. Encourage complete and complex responses
I. Use different types of questions and encourage all children
J. Use to stimulate basic process skills for young children (ages 5 to 10)
K. Use to stimulate integrated process skills for older children (ages 11 and beyond)

IV. How Can You Improve Your Questioning?

A. Training - read, plan , execute questioning strategies
B. Practice - record, analyze, set improvement goals, work toward goals (Table 10.3)

T10.14 V. Why Use Children's Questions?

A. Why bother?
   1. insight into conception and interest
   2. help set realistic expectations
   3. helps children develop habit of reflection

T10.15

B. How can you stimulate children's questions?
   1. stimulate through direct contact with interesting materials and through experiences, child sharing
   2. model good question asking in real time and by visual aids and learning stations (Fig. 10.7) and use questions to construct connections among thoughts (Fig. 10.8)
   3. develop atmosphere that encourages productive questions
   4. include children's questions among your teacher evaluation techniques
   5. use a response strategy that encourages, nurtures and improves children's questions (Fig 10.9)

Chapter 11 Outline

HOW CAN YOU USE SCIENCE DEMONSTRATIONS AND TEXTBOOKS EFFECTIVELY?

Overview T11.0

One study reports that 90 percent of our country's science teachers use a textbook 95 percent of the time. A simple conclusion could be that this is completely bad. Undesirable? Yes. Completely bad? No. Textbooks have undergone some wonderful improvements in the last couple of decades, although some of the research reported in the chapter shows a decline in inclusion and quality on several factors. What is unfortunate is the complete reliance on a single source that is most probably out of date. The Chinese proverb: I hear and I forget, I see and I remember and I do and I understand points out some other possible inadequacies when instruction is focused on one or two ways of learning. Our mission in this chapter is to acknowledge that texts do play a large role in elementary and middle school science and that they can be quite effective when supplemented or reorganized by an enterprising teacher. This chapter introduces readers to effective ways of using teacher demonstrations, improved ways to use exposition through advance organizers, deduction and explicit teaching, and techniques for selecting and using textbooks more effectively.

Content

T11.1 I. How Can You Use Teacher Demonstrations Effectively?

A. Tips for effective demonstrations
1. have a specific, clear purpose
2. plan carefully and practice the demonstration
3. involve children in the demonstration safely
4. support the demonstration with effective questions
5. repeat to focus attention and to help make mental connections
6. use simple, familiar materials
7. keep the demonstration visible
8. connect the demonstration to science goals
9. rely on quality, not quantity

T11.2 B. When should you use a demonstration?
1. to avoid putting the children in danger
2. to model proper skills or safety techniques
3. to focus the class on an important event or concept
4. to over come equipment shortages

T11.3
5. to arouse interest, raise important questions, or pose learning problems
6. to help solve academic problems

7. to apply what has been learned to a new situation
8. to encourage learners who are slower and to challenge rapid learners

T11.4 C. When should children do a demonstration?
1. to recognize effort and originality
2. to help another child understand
3. to enhance or to develop communication skills
4. to build self-confidence

II. How Can You Use Exposition Effectively?
A. Uses
1. use an Advance Organizer before the lesson to help form mental structures
2. use exposition to provide clear instructions
3. use for summary or closure of a lesson
4. use to clarify the explanation phase of the science learning cycle

T11.5 B. Deduction (Fig 11.2)
T11.6 1. Step 1: give the general concept or conclusion of the lesson
2. Step 2: clarify any key terms students may not understand
3. Step 3: give clear examples of the concept or conclusion
4. Step 4: have students obtain experience with the concept or conclusion by working with problems and by giving specific examples

T11.7 C. Explicit Teaching (Table 11.1)
1. begin lesson with brief goal statement
2. give a brief overview of the previous lesson
3. present new material in small steps, practice after each step
4. give clear instructions and explanations
5. provide active practice for all
6. check for understanding, use questioning
7. guide children through practice
8. provide feedback systematically for all children
9. provide explicit instruction and practice, monitor progress
10. continue practice until children master the material

T11.8 III. How Can You Use Science Textbooks Effectively?
A. Be aware of shortcomings and differences relevant to:
1. focus
2. science goals that are addressed
3. clarity and function of illustrations
4. end-of-chapter supplements
5. uses of inquiry approaches
6. inclusion of activities or experiments

B. Enhance the text
  1. supplement with material from old editions and from publishers of similar materials
  2. supplement from experimental programs
  3. use local resources
  4. consult with state department of education
  5. screen for appropriate reading level
  6. select proper evaluation devices
  7. organize teachers to form supplement teams
  8. attend professional conferences to learn new ideas
  9. focus on concepts and processes

T11.9 C. Change the sequence (Fig 11.3, 11.4, Table 11.2)
  1. proceed from smallest to largest ideas
  2. show how ideas or concepts are interrelated
  3. make the content structure clear to your students

D. Selecting the best textbook (Tables 11.3, 11.4)
  1. examine purpose and compare to intent of your science program
  2. examine reading level and compare to ability of students
  3. examine text for extent to which it addresses important science goals
  4. examine the types of thinking students will be required to do
  5. examine for the extent to which process skills are developed
  6. examine for conceptual focus

TEST ITEM BANK

Chapter 1
WHAT IS SCIENCE?
Test Items

THE FOLLOWING ARE **MULTIPLE CHOICE** QUESTIONS. Select the single best answer for each question.

1.1. When looking at results of the National Assessment of Educational Progress for grades 4, 8, and 12 some definite trends can be detected. One trend discovered is that:

A) At all grade levels over 50% of the students are capable of analyzing scientific procedures and data.
B) Only at the 12th grade level are we successful at having students understand simple scientific principles.
C) Over 50% of students within grades 4, 8, and 12 are capable of integrating specialized scientific information.
D) American students at all grade levels assessed are quite successful at understanding simple scientific principles - of answering pure knowledge types of questions about science.
E) None of the above.

1.2. Teachers who allow their students to participate in scientific investigation, reflect upon data collected, share with one another, relate their findings to scientific achievements and careers, and study and use many different sources for collecting and analyzing data are:

A) Having students experience the excitement of science.
B) Exposing the students to possible career choices related to science.
C) Preparing students to be able to work with others and learn to accept ideas of others.
D) Creating a need for the uses of present-day technology.
E) All of the above.

1.3. Ms. Smith, a kindergarten teacher was sharing a *Where's Waldo* book with her students. They spent time searching for Waldo and for many other objects in each picture. After this activity Ms. Smith had the students create their own hidden picture pages to share with their peers. A parent in her class was later heard to complain that his child did too many games in school and when were they going to learn real things like Science and Mathematics? Which of the following is a valid argument for Ms. Smith to give that parent about her *Where's Waldo* lesson?

A) The students were having fun and my job as a kindergarten teacher is to make sure they feel good about school and have fun.
B) Science is more than just products. It is also attitudes and processes. I was helping develop the process skill of observing.
C) Since there is no current *Model Curriculum* for Science in this state, I can do whatever I want with my students and call it science.
D) At the kindergarten level I'm not required to teach science or mathematics.
E) The students will find out soon enough that subjects like science and mathematics are hard. Right now I just want them to feel good about school.

1.4. Ms. Bateman walked into her science class with an inflated balloon and a large needle sticking right through it. The students were intrigued and excited all at once. She asked for their ideas on why they think the balloon didn't pop. She broke them into groups to determine why the balloon didn't pop. Which group of students truly understands what it means to be a scientist?

A) Group A spent their entire planning time scanning their textbook in hope of finding the right answer.

B) Group B collected various sizes and thickness' of balloons and stuck the needle through each of them once inflated. They made observations and took notes about how each balloon reacted when the needle was pushed in at different spots.

C) Group C went to the library to look through the encyclopedia for an answer.

D) Group D got on the internet hoping to reach a local scientist who could give them the answer.

E) None of the above.

1.5. Which of the following teachers prove s/he understands what it means to be scientifically literate?

A) Ms. Kaufman engaged her sixth grade students in an experiment, but not without first telling them everything to do exactly and what results they should obtain.

B) Mr. Carlson had his eighth grade students created study guides in which the students quizzed one another on a list of scientific terms. All of his students were able to repeat the definitions of several scientific terms.

C) Mrs. Williams had every student in her third grade class participate in the school science fair. Many of the projects were models of volcanoes or the solar system.

D) Ms. Helkey, with the help of her first grade students, decided that the entire week would be dedicated to studying the ocean. Everything the children did that week was linked to the ocean. Science investigations were designed so that mathematics and computer skills were necessary to complete the investigation.

E) None of the above.

1.6. If nothing else, the story of George deMestral's discovery of velcro, teaches students that:

A) Observing the commonplace can provide important insights.

B) Science is hard.

C) Recognition for good work comes only when you're older or dead.

D) Discovery and invention are synonymous.

E) Discoveries are just a matter of luck.

1.7. Which of the following scenarios suggest that the students are engaged in a whole science experience?

A) Mrs. A's class has just finished a hike in the land lab. They are in the process of identifying specimens that Mrs. A handed them while out doors. She indicated that a prize will be given for the group that finishes keying out their specimens first, especially if they have all of the genus and species names correctly identified.

B) Mr. J's class started an experiment on photosynthesis, but when their plants became all spindly because no one watered them over a long weekend they opted for looking through various resources to find out everything they could about plant photosynthesis.

C) Mr. C's class were asked to make predictions about why the *Efferdent tablets* did not dissolve when dropped in a clear liquid. All of the students were curious because they felt for sure that once placed in water the tablets should begin to dissolve by bubbling and fizzing. None of this occurred so they immediately began to plan experiments to figure out why. After their experimental plans were approved by Mr. C they acted on their ideas, recorded their observations, shared with the class and drew conclusions. As a group they used their experimental results to draw conclusions which explained why Mr. C's tablets didn't dissolve. Mr. C verified the accuracy of their results with additional insights and that led them to another exploration.

D) Ms. K's class also wondered why *Efferdent tablets* didn't dissolve in the clear liquid. They expected them to bubble and fizz and yet that didn't happen even after they suggested to Ms. K that she crumble up the tablet first. After that suggestion was tried Ms. K told the class that not all clear liquids are water and that not all clear liquids behave like water. She asked the class to make predictions about what the clear liquid could be and then she stopped soliciting answers once she received the correct answer, alcohol.

E) None of the teachers were able to engage their students in a whole science experience.

1.8. Which of the following would not be an intellectual attitude to develop in a child in your science class?

A) A desire for reliable sources of information.
B) Avoidance of broad generalizations when evidence is limited.
C) Refusal to believe in superstitions or to accept claims without proof.
D) Intolerance for other opinions, explanations, or points of view.
E) Skepticism; a desire to be shown or to have alternative points of view proven.

1.9. Curiosity, perseverance, cooperation and open-mindedness are characteristic of what kind of scientific attitudes?

A. intellectual
B. positive
C. emotional
D. innate
E. adult

1.10. Through observation, organization, classification, and communication, students learn

A. basic skills and information
B. to think critically and to use information creatively
C. to obtain information as it is needed
D. the scientific method
E. intellectual attitudes

1.11. Charlie was curious as to which brand of dishwashing soap blew the best bubbles. To determine which was the best he designed an experiment so that all of the soap solutions were made in exactly the same manner except for using different brands. He made sure that he did at least three trials for each brand, thoroughly cleaned his surface in between brands, used a clean bubble blower for each brand, and took extra care not to contaminate soap samples. He made accurate measurements of soap rings left by the popped bubble and recorded these precisely. Which integrated process skill was Charlie using?

A) Observing
B) Controlling Variables

C) Graphing
D) Inferring
E) Measuring

The following are TRUE or FALSE. On your answer sheet, mark letter A for true and letter B for false.

1.12. Even today, it is not uncommon for children to picture most scientists as male.

1.13. Most teachers report that their teaching goal for science should primarily emphasize basic science concepts.

1.14. Time allotted for science teaching has not increased significantly in the past 15 years.

1.15. Science, as defined in our class, consists of science knowledge, processes, and attitudes.

1.16 - 1.33 An understanding of scientific attitudes, process skills, and science knowledge is essential to effective science teaching. Correctly identify the following aspects of science as:
A = Attitude, B = Process, C = Science Knowledge

1.16. objectivity
1.17. generalizations
1.18. observing
1.19. communicating
1.20. defining operationally
1.21. curiosity
1.22. skepticism
1.23. controlling variables
1.24. principles
1.25. predicting
1.26. open-mindedness
1.27. theories
1.28. hypothesizing
1.29. inferring
1.30. evaluating
1.31. concepts
1.32. identifying problems
1.33. measuring

CHAPTER 1
Answer Key for Test Items

1.1	D	1.2	E	1.3	B	1.4	B	1.5	D	1.6	A	1.7	C
1.8	D	1.9	C	1.10	A	1.11	B	1.12	A	1.13	A	1.14	A
1.15	A												

1.16.	objectivity	A
1.17.	generalizations	C
1.18.	observing	B
1.19.	communicating	B
1.20.	defining operationally	B
1.21.	curiosity	A
1.22.	skepticism	A
1.23.	controlling variables	B
1.24.	principles	C
1.25.	predicting	B
1.26.	open-mindedness	A
1.27.	theories	C
1.28.	hypothesizing	B
1.29.	inferring	B
1.30.	evaluating	B
1.31.	concepts	C
1.32.	identifying problems	B
1.33.	measuring	B

Chapter 2
HOW DO CHILDREN LEARN SCIENCE?
Test Items

THE FOLLOWING ARE **MULTIPLE CHOICE** QUESTIONS. Select the single best answer for each question.

2.1. Which of the following teachers demonstrate that they know what children need in order to help them learn?

A) Walking into Mr. Yarborough's classroom you find it filled with live animals. The students are responsible for maintaining cages, feeding, and showing concern for the animals. Not only does he use the various animal maintenance chores as a way of building student confidence, but he also ties in many of his science lessons to the animals. Today you observe the students moving around the classroom constantly, many are talking to one another actively solving problems about a certain animal's feeding behavior. If a group of students gets heavily involved in solving a problem which deals with the animals, Mr. Yarborough gives the students the time they need during class to work out their problems.

B) Upon entering Mrs. Peele's classroom you observe rows of quiet students filling out a science workbook page. After the students have been given a reasonable amount of time to complete the paper Mrs. Peele then goes over it with them. The students know all of the science concepts on the page.

C) Ms. Hernandez has prepared enough materials so that every child in her class may do today's activity alone. The children are working quietly by themselves to find a solution to a science problem. After sufficient time had passed, Ms. Hernandez collected whatever the students wrote and without any sharing of papers, simply recorded a score to the science problem.

D) All of the above.

E) None of the above.

2.2. Which of the following is true of constructivism?

A) It is a synthesis of several dominant perspectives on learning.

B) In this theory the learner "re-invents the wheel", yet retains information better with a deeper understanding.

C) A downside is that students may construct misconceptions and the teacher needs to step in and correct those.

D) It assumes that knowledge is a construction of reality.

E) All of the above.

2.3 Jamie once witnessed a discrepant event in which the teacher had placed some raisins into a glass of 7-up and the teacher pretended the raisins, which were moving up and down in the pop, were *sewer lice*. Jamie and his peers were to determine if the *sewer lice* were indeed living since they showed movement. On the day the students did the experiment Jamie was absent. By the time he returned to school the teacher had moved on to teach other characteristics of living things. Jamie never did get the message that there were no such things as *sewer lice*. The biggest danger of leaving Jamie with this misconception is that:

A) He will think that anything that is brown and moves up and down is sewer lice.

B) He will not believe anyone who tells him that *sewer lice* do not exist, even when they share evidence which proves it, since the evidence Jamie has constructed contradicts theirs.

C) Jamie will never eat raisins again.
D) He will not be able to list all of the characteristics of living things.
E) There is no danger, eventually he will discover that *sewer lice* don't exist.

2.4. Which of the following teachers best demonstrates Constructivist Teaching Strategies?

A) Mrs. Smith read the story *The Giving Tree* to her fourth grade students and had them share their feelings about the story. They then engaged in an exploratory activity of making paper from recycled paper they had been saving in their classroom. After the exploration the teacher, with the student's help, invented the concept - *Used paper can be recycled to make new paper.* The students then engaged in another activity which was a letter writing campaign using, the newly made paper, to encourage policy makers in their community to urge all citizens to recycle. Mrs. Smith evaluated her students based on the their ability to demonstrate to her how to make paper from recycled paper, and on the quality of the arguments the students used in their letters to local policy makers.

B) Mrs. Carlson spent several days with her third grade students reading to them about the life cycle of various insects. She then had them go outdoors and each collect 10 insects. They were given a grade on how well the identified and displayed each insect.

C) Mr. Cortez took his sixth grade students to the local museum of natural history to study dinosaurs. While going through the dinosaur displays each student was required to answer questions on a worksheet concerning the dinosaurs. The students were to check one another's answers in the bus on the way home. The next day Mr. Cortez gave the students a quiz on the information they learned from the field trip.

D) Ms. Kelly's first grade course of study identified magnetism as a concept to be taught. To meet this objective Ms. Kelly presented a lesson on magnetism to her first graders. She had one magnet which she showed the students and proceeded to demonstrate how magnets can pick up objects. After her demonstration she gave each child a handout page with pictures of objects like a key, a baseball, a can, etc... on it. She asked each child to circle which objects will be attracted to a magnet. The next day her science lesson was on plants.

E) Mr. Strong's lesson on rocks and minerals to his fifth grade students started with a lecture on what would happen to anyone if they were caught throwing any of the rocks in his classroom. After that lecture he called upon different students to read the pages from the textbook out loud. When the students came to an activity in the chapter Mr. Strong stopped and talked about what would happen if they were to do the activity. After his brief explanation he continued calling on students until they reached the end of the chapter. Mr. Strong then assigned the questions at the end of the chapter with a warning that all of the questions were to be completed by the end of class as the students were going to be tested on that information the next day.

2.5. Upon entering the science classroom, the third grade students found the following item at their work stations: a capped two-liter bottle filled with water with a medicine (eye) dropper floating inside. Printed instructions asked the students to squeeze the sides of the bottles and observe the effects; the dropper sank deeper in the water the harder the children squeezed the bottle. A constructivist science educator would ask which question of the students as they were squeezing the bottle?

A) Why does the dropper sink?

B) What physical processes are taking place inside the bottle?

C) What do you observe happening in the bottle?

D) What scientific principle is involved in this demonstration?

E) Why do the droppers sink and rise as you adjust the pressure on the bottles?

2.6. Samantha asked her teacher, *"Why do some things float and others sink?"* How could Samantha's teacher best answer the question so that the principles of **constructivism** are used?

A) Set up a demonstration on why things float and have the class discuss it.

B) Help Samantha do an experiment to determine for herself why things float.

C) Tell Samantha the answer and have her obtain more information on the topic and report back to the rest of the class.

D) Have Samantha look up the answer in her science book.

E) Just make up something because Samantha will never know anyway.

2.7. The teacher's method in developing a scientific approach to problem-solving is reflected in the children's learning. Which of the following is an approach which exemplifies problem-solving?

A) Let the students first try to solve teacher-defined problems they encounter themselves without teacher guidance.

B) Try to think and see things as a child thinks and sees.

C) Encourage students to be creative even though it may mean more problems for the teacher.

D) Strive to cover a definite amount of information in the time allowed.

E) Determine the children's interest and help them identify science problems they value. Guide them as they seek to investigate the solve the problems for themselves.

2.8. A teacher turns a glass tumbler containing a wad of paper inside it upside down and pushes the rim straight down into a clear container filled with water. Which of the following teaching techniques would indicate that the teacher believes it is important to build upon children's prior knowledge and experiences?

A) The teacher explains that air occupies space and gives examples such as blowing up a balloon or asking children to demonstrate the difficulty in trying to compress the extended plunger of a sealed plastic syringe. The teacher then asks the children to predict what will happen to the paper when the inverted glass is immersed in water.

B) The teacher does the experiment again and asks the children to take notes on what happens.

C) The teacher repeats the experiment, allows the children to comment on their observations, and then gives them her own explanation.

D) Before the teacher does the experiment, she asks the children what they think will happen. She does the experiment and then asks children to check their guess with what they observed. She then asks for comments on the reasons for the phenomena.

MATCH the views on constructivism with the statement which closest represents that point of view. These include:

A = Radical Constructivist **B = Conservative Constructivist**

C = Traditionalists

2.9. Knowledge cannot exist outside the mind of a thinking person. Knowledge is a representation of reality that is made by each learner.

2.10. Learning should occur inductively, that is, provide children with activities to help them see the underlying ideas, concepts, relationships, and patterns in science.

2.11. Every time you teach a child something, you keeps him or her from reinventing it, that is, you keep the child from forming mental schemes to accommodate or assimilate the experience.

2.12. Learning occurs mentally and an advance mental organizer enables the learner to put to use that more readily which is learned.

2.13. Children learn physically and mentally through personal struggles where they must investigate.

2.14. Science is composed of many facts, principles, theories, which must be mastered before new material can be learned

2.15. Teachers must teach in a way to help children to form mental structures and to grasp the structures of the science discipline.

2.16. Children's interactions with the environment provides mental conflicts which create dilemmas. These dilemmas motivate children to restore mental equilibrium.

2.17. Learning is dependent upon developing a framework of specific concepts and the teacher helping the student form connections between those concepts.

2.18. Children's prior ideas affect present learning. Existing conceptions can enhance or limit new concept formation.

2.19. Children learn best by doing and reflecting on what they do.

2.20. Most elementary children need to manipulate concrete materials in order to explain a scientific phenomenon. They are not ready for more abstract thought processes.

2.21. Children learn best by allowing only their minds to act on what is being learned. This can be done by listening, speaking, reading, seeing, and thinking.

2.22. The most important single factor influencing learning is what the learner already knows.

2.23. Children learn by forming mental structures. As a child ages the his/her ability to understand abstract concepts will increase.

2.24. In learning socialization is important to assure that there is a purpose to student activity.

2.25. Learning best occurs by starting with specific student experiences and guiding the student's thinking to form the concept or general idea.

As supported by the constructivist perspective, which of the following are suggestions for facilitating the development of children's intellect and skills?
Use **A = Agree** and **D = Disagree**.

2.26. Emphasize "hands-on," concrete activities in all grades.

2.27. Restrict the freedom for children to choose their own learning activities because a basic core of science must be learned.

2.28. Attempt the determine the ideas children bring to science class with them in an effort to help them avoid misconceptions.

2.29. Design specific questions and learning tasks to facilitate the development of certain science process skills, e.g., observation, classification, measurement, communication, etc.

2.30. Interact with individual children to determine how and what they think.

2.31. Introduce concepts or use abstract technical terms after children have a concrete reference such as a hands-on experience.

2.32. Try an "explore, explain, expand and evaluate" teaching and learning approach.

Match the following teacher roles as a constructivist educator with the appropriate description. Use these answers.
A = Presenter **B = Observer** **C = Question Asker/Problem Poser** **D = Environment Organizer** **E = Public Relations Coordinator**

2.33. Works to identify children's prior ideas.

2.34. Encourages cooperation rather than competition.

2.35. Designs activities necessary for a child to grow, mature and develop the tools for productive learning.

2.36. Provides experiences useful for thinking and language development, may model or provide demonstrations of scientific phenomenon.

2.37. Stimulates student's ideas and poses problems which arise from observation.

CHAPTER 2
Answer Key for Test Items

2.1	A	2.2	E	2.3	B	2.4	A	2.5	C	2.6	B	2.7	E
2.8	A	2.9	A	2.10	B	2.11	B	2.12	C	2.13	A	2.14	C
2.15	B	2.16	B	2.17	B	2.18	A	2.19	A	2.20	B	2.21	T
2.22	A	2.23	B	2.24	A	2.25	B	2.26	A	2.27	D	2.28	A
2.29	A	2.30	A	2.31	A	2.32	A	2.33	B	2.34	E	2.35	D
2.36	A	2.37	C										

Chapter 3
HOW CAN YOU TEACH SCIENCE FOR ALL CHILDREN?
Test Items

THE FOLLOWING ARE **MULTIPLE CHOICE** QUESTIONS. Select the single best answer for each question.

3.1. One of your learning disabled students brought a live praying mantis to your class, not knowing its identity. As an effective classroom teacher which of the following do you believe will assist that student in developing a positive attitude toward learning?
A) Tell the student what it is and ask the student to put it in the back of the room to be shown to the class later.
B) Thank the student for sharing it with you and tell him to let release it outdoors.
C) Set aside your planned lesson and have the student share it with the class. Encourage the students to work together to find out more about the insect by providing him/her with resources to find additional information. Ask the student to share the findings the rest of the class.
D) None of the above because a praying mantis is not included in the curriculum.

3.2. Jose, a student in Mrs. Paul's class, constantly keeps forgetting the instructions for class experiments and forgets to take home his "take-home folder" with each day's assignments. Jose's homework is usually late or incomplete. He has trouble in science class trying to remember the difference between rotation and revolution while studying the movements of planets and moons in the solar system. As her teacher, Mrs. Paul should do which of the following to help Jose?
A) Nothing. Rotation and revolution are not important to Jose, therefore he will never learn it anyway.
B) Make Jose stay after school and help him complete his assignments.
C) Two things: (1) work with Jose to help him become more organized since organization is the key to meeting deadlines, and (2) help Jose make meaningful connections between "rotation" and "revolution" because these connections will help him to understand the concepts.
D) Ask Jose's parents to spend more time with him while he does homework.
E) None of the above

3.3. To instruct a student who has a learning disability, a teacher might best:
A) Enter the student in the science fair to help motivate him/her.
B) Have a gifted child help the student who has the disability.
C) Give additional homework to the learner and keep him/her in from recess so the work gets done.
D) Teach so that as many of the senses as possible are used.
E) None of the above; just help the student who has the learning disability to get by.

3.4. Which of the following teachers best demonstrates that she/he is teaching to overcome gender inequalities in science education?
A) Mr. Smith has divided the class into competitive work teams of males and females thinking that same gender teams will perform better.
B) Ms. Lincoln has worked as a research scientist and tries to bring in her work experiences in her teaching, encouraging all students to participate in

science activities.

C) Mrs. Juliani created science information bulletin boards, purchasing ready made science posters that featured all males in white lab coats.

D) Mr. Clark carefully searched for a textbook that was gender neutral and then just lectured from that for the entire school year to avoid exposing the students to any gender biased materials.

E) Ms. Athanapolous engaged her students in science activities, yet frequently assigned the females the role of record keeper and materials person. The males were asked to lead the activity team and to report on their results more often than females.

3.5. Which of the following parents best demonstrates that she/he is assisting her/his child in studying and preparing for science?

A) Mrs. Lopez tells her daughter that she was never any good at mathematics so it's okay if her daughter isn't either.

B) Mr. Johanson sits with his son each evening thoroughly explaining each science concept and expecting his son to give detailed descriptions of each concept once the father finishes his lecture.

C) Ms. Witmer asks her son if he's having any difficulty with his science or mathematics and then asks how she can help with the problem. Together they try to resolve the difficulty the son is having.

D) Mr. Clay has no idea when and if his daughter has mathematics or science homework. Most nights he lets her go out to play right after school and watch television in the evening. Little or no homework is ever completed.

E) Ms. Ames expects her children to sit for two hours each evening to do homework. Even if they have no assignments she makes them read something for two hours. They are discouraged from talking to one another during this time and are expected to have all work completed by the end of the two hours.

3.6. Children who show promise of making superior progress in school are labeled:

A) LD

B) Behavior Disorder

C) Talented and Gifted

D) Achievers

E) All of the Above

3.7. Mr. Beverlin taught elementary school in an area with a large percentage of students from foreign countries., He was constantly searching through references trying to find examples of scientific phenomenon which his international students could relate to. Which of the following best reflects Mr. Beverlin's philosophy of science teaching?

A) Access to science information is important.

B) Selected teaching materials and methods should reflect and incorporate diversity.

C) Not all students learn the same, therefore how I instruct them may have to vary among students.

D) All of the above.

E) None of the above.

3.8 - 3.21 Indicate whether each of the following is true or false. Use:
A = True and B = False

3.8. Parents, teachers, school counselors, and peers discourage females from pursuing scientific careers.

3.9. While engaged in science processes the teacher must never expect the same behaviors from females as males.

3.10. Placing a hearing impaired child into a cooperative learning group can result in isolation for the hearing impaired child.

3.11. Public Law 04-142 of 1975 is part of a federal law which helps insure a place for handicapped students in American public schools.

3.12. Concept analysis is a strategy that has great potential for assisting a child with a learning disability to succeed in school.

3.13. All children are culturally diverse.

3.14 The 1991 position statement on multicultural science education urges teachers to become aware of children's learning styles and instructional preferences.

3.15 It is easier for children to understand and accept cultural differences if these differences are ignored at early ages.

3.16. An African American child who is from a poor home environment is envisioned as a typical example of the culturally different.

3.17. Advocates of multicultural education believe that the needs of all children differ and that these differences should be taken into account.

3.18. Lack of familiarity with the dominant spoken language can cause students to believe their fate is beyond their control.

3.19. Both males and females, by age 11, have developed strong sex-stereotyped attitudes concerning socially appropriate behavior and gender roles in society.

3.20. Parents, teachers, school counselors, should encourage males to pursue non-traditional careers in scientific fields, i.e.., nursing, medical secretary.

3.21. A shortage of appropriate female science and engineering role models reinforces the belief that science is only for males.

CHAPTER 3
Answer Key for Test Items

3.1	C	3.2	C	3.3	D	3.4	B	3.5	C	3.6	C	3.7	D
3.8	A	3.9	B	3.10	A	3.11	A	3.12	A	3.13	A	3.14	A
3.15	B	3.16	A	3.17	A	3.18	A	3.19	A	3.20	A	3.21	A

Chapter 4
WHAT GOALS PROMOTE SCIENTIFIC LITERACY?
Test Items

THE FOLLOWING ARE **MULTIPLE CHOICE** QUESTIONS. Select the single best answer for each question.

4.1. Jordan is a fourth grade student that was saddled with the reputation of being inattentive, a poor reader, and a discipline problem. His third grade teacher warned Ms. Tuttle, his fourth grade teacher, that it was rare for Jordan to ever pick up a book on his own and even rarer for Jordan to want to work with any other students. Ms. Tuttle, was not ready to simply accept the horror stories shared by his third grade teacher. Ms. Tuttle had some new fish in her classroom. She decided to assign Jordan the responsibility of caring for those fish for the first quarter of the school year. She taught Jordan how to feed them, and she suggested that every time he fed the fish he should first tap on the glass in one specific spot. Toward the end of the first quarter the class was covering characteristics of living things. One characteristic discussed was the ability to respond to a stimulus. Once that characteristic was mentioned Ms. Tuttle asked Jordan to go over and feed the fish while the rest of the class watched. Jordan was a bit confused and reluctantly did as Ms. Tuttle asked. Of course, by this time, as soon as Jordan knocked on that one specific spot on the fish tank, the fish came swimming over, ready to be fed. The class was amazed. Many children asked Jordan how he did that. Jordan simply told them that by tapping his hand in one specific spot he was getting the fish to respond. He explained to the students how his tapping in one spot helped train the fish. Many other questions were asked of Jordan about how long it took him to get the fish to do this. By the time the students had exhausted their questions about the fish Ms. Tuttle determined that her students understood many characteristics of living things. She thanked Jordan for assisting her in teaching the class. Jordan beamed with pride. Later in the day Jordan was found sharing a book on fish with a some fellow students. They were overheard planning a date to the local fish store together. Which statement below describes the belief Ms. Tuttle has about science teaching?

A) Science concepts should only be taught if they have practical applications.
B) Science is taught best when students read about concepts first before they perform experiments.
C) Science teaching can provide opportunities to develop positive attitudes toward learning.
D) Not all children are capable of learning science concepts.
E) Science teaching should not be used to teach reading skills.

4.2. Which of the following questions would you ask a child if your were trying to assist the child in understanding how the concept of *states of matter* could help him/her in his/her personal development?

A) What are the states of matter?
B) What kind of a job would require you to know about the differences between states of matter?
C) How is a gas different from a liquid?
D) How important is it to understand how water can be in a solid or liquid state of matter if you were responsible for building roads?
E) How important do you think it is to be able to freeze water? What do you create by changing matter this way?

4.3. You are interviewing for a teaching position. The principal is proud of the elementary school's science program and asks: "What goals are most important for a science program?" To show you are aware of the mission of elementary science you should reply by saying:

A) To provide science learning experiences that help fill students' personal as well as social needs.
B) To provide science learning experiences that help students learn to distinguish between natural objects and objects made by humans.
C) To provide science learning experiences that provide academic preparation through inquiry to teach specific science concepts and skills.
D) To provide science learning experiences that help students become aware of career opportunities which rely on science and the historical nature of science.
E) All of the above.

4.4. What evidence supports the claim that science helps promote basic skill development?

A) Science helps to increase reading and language skills and to expand general knowledge.
B) Science helps to increase a child's understanding of mathematics concepts and number skills.
C) Science process skills and reading skills promote development of the same thought processes.
D) Science helps to promote creative thinking and positive attitudes.
E) All of the above may be true.

4.5 One of the first major research projects that indicated that most of science teaching in schools was in telling children about what scientists did rather than allowing children to experience what scientists do was:

A) Project Synthesis
B) Scope, Sequence, and Coordination of Secondary School Science
C) Project 2061
D) National Research Council Science Education Standards
E) Goals 2000

4.6 - 4.17. The goals for effective elementary science instruction provide a foundation for planning. The goals for science education cluster around four dimensions for science teaching. Indicate which of the goals below match the following dimensions by marking:

A = Personal and Social Perspectives
B = Science and Technology
C = Science as Inquiry
D = History and Nature of Science

4.6. Students will recognize that the solution to one problem can create new problems and that scientists and engineers must work together with their technological designs to solve problems.

4.7. The students will recognize that data may be interpreted differently by different people depending on their values and experiences.

4.8. The students will develop an awareness of the occupational and professional opportunities for women, minorities and the handicapped in science.

4.9. The students will learn to think critically, creatively and rationally so they can solve problems and promote life-long academic learning.

4.10. The students will develop process skills so that they can think scientifically.

4.11. The students will develop a knowledge and understanding of scientific principles and concepts.

4.12. The students will realize that the size of human and animal population can increase or decrease and that populations will increase unless factors such as disease limit it.

4.13. The students will develop an understanding of the capacities and limits of man made tools.

4.14. The students will develop problem-solving skills that they need to survive in a changing world.

4.15. The students will recognize how the advancement of science and technology has changed the lives of people.

4.16. The students will develop skills as well as effective and positive work habits related to scientific careers.

4.17. The students will understand and use new ideas and scientific information to improve their lives.

4.18 - 4.23. Many major science improvement efforts have suggested goals for effective science teaching. Indicate if you agree that the following are recommended goals by marking: **A = Agree** and **D = Disagree**.

4.18. Science curricula should include content that deals with social issues and technology when possible.

4.19. Science teachers should prepare students who can understand the nature of science and its way of knowing.

4.20. Science teaching should provide students with information about scientific phenomenon whether it has meaning to them at this point in their life or not.

4.21. The use of textbooks should be limited.

4.22. The teachers for each school district should be allowed to determine the goals of science education.

4.23. Effective science instruction must encourage student diversity and serve the needs and interests of all students with a common core of knowledge and experiences.

CHAPTER 4
Answer Key for Test Items

4.1	C	4.2	E	4.3	E	4.4	E	4.5	A	4.6	B	4.7	A
4.8	D	4.9	C	4.10	C	4.11	C	4.12	A	4.13	B	4.14	C
4.15	B	4.16	D	4.17	A	4.18	A	4.19	A	4.20	D	4.21	A
4.22	D	4.23	A										

Chapter 5
HOW CAN YOU PLAN CONSTRUCTIVIST SCIENCE LESSONS AND ASSESS STUDENT PERFORMANCE?
Test Items

THE FOLLOWING ARE **MULTIPLE CHOICE** QUESTIONS. Select the single best answer for each question.

5.1. Ms. Jules felt that doing activity based science with twenty-seven students in her class was impossible. Her biggest complaint was that there was no organized manner to record what the students really knew. Which of her colleagues provided her with the best argument against her complaint?
- A) Ms. Rotel told her that she could just do an activity every other week and that would make it easier to keep track of what the students knew.
- B) Mr. Hempstead stated that even though you did science activities with your students you could still give multiple choice/fill in the blank tests to determine what they learned.
- C) Ms. Copertino stated that it really was easy to keep track of the concepts or skills the children were learning, and then provided Ms. Jules with a systematic observation guide she used in her class and showed Ms. Jules how to use it.
- D) Ms. Polel said to use cooperative groups and to give them worksheets which the students filled out together and turned in to the teacher for a grade.
- E) Mrs. Hartman felt it best to ask the students to turn in a sheet of paper at the end of each class stating how they felt about today's lesson. She stated that gave her a pretty good idea of what her students learned for the day.

5.2. The purpose of a portfolio is:
- A) for the teacher to keep graded papers on each student in one folder.
- B) to tell a story about the student's science achievements.
- C) to keep track of student achievement through teacher anecdotal records.
- D) for the student to keep track of teacher comments on student work.
- E) none of the above.

5.3. Concept maps provide the greatest benefit to:
- A) the teacher.
- B) the student .
- C) both teacher and student.
- D) curriculum director.
- E) none of the above.

5.4. Which of the following is the best representation of a performance objective? The children should:
- A) When given certain data, be able to predict the outcome of an investigation within a reasonable amount of accuracy.
- B) Be able to better appreciate air pollution.
- C) Develop an understanding of kinetic energy.
- D) Be more receptive to logical presentations of conclusions based on data.

5.5. In devising appropriate evaluation procedures for science teaching, which of the following should be considered before you begin?
- A) Does the procedure you select or develop actually determine the child's

ability to function, understand, problem-solve, and/or appreciate science?

B) Is there enough time to develop and to have the children complete an appropriate form of evaluation?

C) Should evaluation be done during the lessons or at the end of the unit of instruction?

D) Do I have adequate equipment for doing a performance evaluation?

E) Should I use the test supplied with the text or science program or develop my own?

5.6. One important reason for using pictures with questions in a science classroom is that they:

A) Help to create interest.

B) Help students apply what they learn.

C) Provide a useful alternative evaluation tool (pictorial assessment).

D) Can provide for an inquiring learning situation.

E) Give students something to look at when they don't know the answers.

5.7. Student misconceptions can be revealed to the teacher most easily through

A) Student discussion and essay questions.

B) Supply item tests.

C) Fill-in-the-blank tests.

D) Matching tests.

E) None of the above.

5.8. *Like poles of a magnet repel each other and opposite poles attract.* This statement is an example of a:

A) Fact

B) Concept

C) Goal

D) Generalization

E) Objective

5.9. Water has weight is an example of a:

A) Fact

B) Concept

C) Goal

D) Generalization

E) Objective

5.10 - 5.14 Which of the following are examples of clearly written concept statements in elementary science?

Use: **A = Agree and D = Disagree.**

5.10. Knowing about the effects of oil spills is important.

5.11. Air takes up space and can be used to do work.

5.12. The earth rotates on its axis once in approximately 24 hours.

5.13. There are many facts known about the moon.

5.14. Excluding air friction, objects fall at the same rate regardless of mass, size, or shape.

5.15 - 5.27 The following questions pertain to concept mapping.
Use: **A= True and B = False.**

5.15. A concrete graphic illustration that indicates how a single concept is related to other concepts can be called a concept map.

5.16. Misconceptions may be identified and corrected when concepts maps are student generated.

5.17. Concepts maps are a useful tool for making decisions about the scope of the concepts a teacher should cover in an instructional program.

5.18. Concept maps are the same as brainstorm webs.

5.19. Concept maps do not present ideas in a related hierarchy.

5.20. Concept maps help children to fit new ideas into a meaningful pattern.

5.21. Concept maps may be used as Advance Organizers for science lessons.

5.22. Concept maps may be used as a form of student evaluation.

5.23. Subordinate concepts are located at the top of the map and represent the main, over-arching idea.

5.24. Superordinate concepts are located under and are related to the Subordinate Concept.

5.25. Propositions function as linking words which show how subordinate concepts are related to superordinate concepts.

5.26. Facts are single ideas or descriptions which have no predictive value and may be located at the lowest level of the concept map.

5.27. Coordinating concepts are subordinate concepts, but are only found on the first level of the map's hierarchy under the superordinate concept.

5.28 - 5.34 The following statements are concerned with assessment.
Use: **A = Agree and D = Disagree.**

5.28. In an authentic assessment the person being examined will be able to ask questions of the examiner while being assessed.

5.29. Rote learning methods will be successful if a school district uses authentic assessment to look at achievement.

5.30. Authentic assessment looks for habits of mind rather than habits of recall.

5.31. Authentic assessment is more costly to implement than the more traditional forms of assessment.

5.32. Reflective questions will require students to use their knowledge in a way that is different from the way it was experienced in the lesson.

5.33. Teachers engaged in using constructivist teaching strategies will create assessment instruments which simply have reflective types of questions.

5.34. A well-made teacher test for science will have not only a hands-on section, but also pictorial and reflective types of questions.

5.35 - 5.38. A group of children in Ms. Harper's class successfully created the concept of a circuit. After they had a chance to manipulate batteries, bulbs, and wires, they announced that they could determine if any arrangement of bulbs, wires, and batteries would work. Kevin, a classmate in another group, decided to challenge them. He handed them some diagrams of batteries, bulbs, and wires arranged as circuits. Kevin asked them to determine which of the following arrangements will cause the bulb to light. Help that group meet Kevin's challenge. Indicate with an **A** if you **agree** that arrangement will light the bulb, and with a **D** if you determine the bulb **will not light**.
Use A = agree **D = disagree**

5.35.

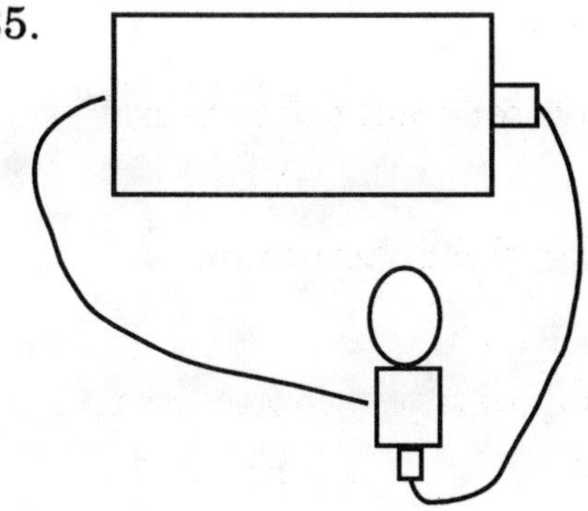

5.36

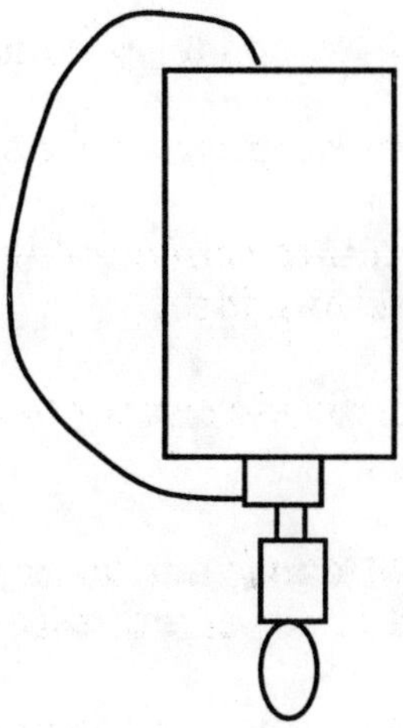

5.37

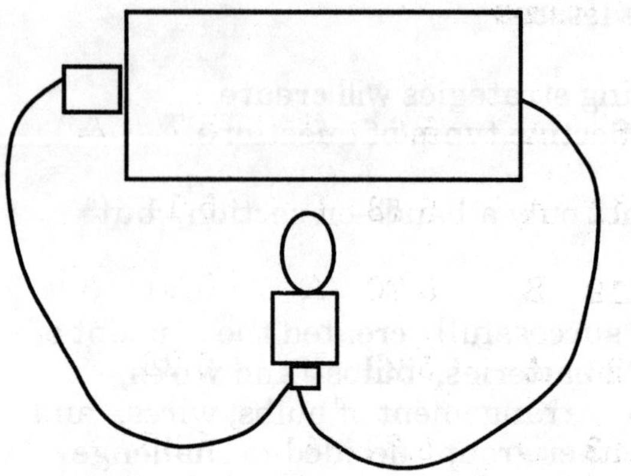

5.38

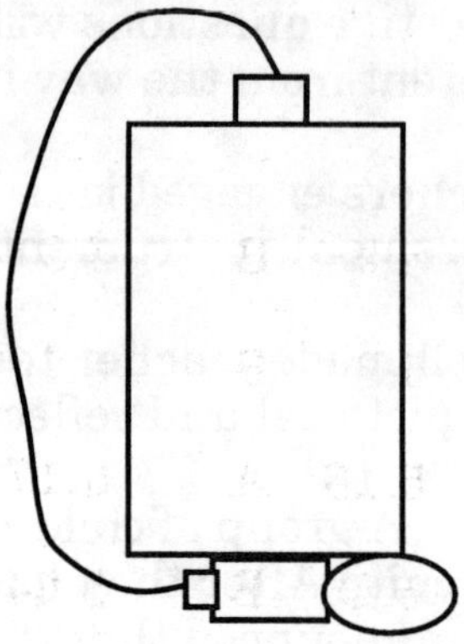

CHAPTER 5
Answer Key for Test Items

5.1 C	5.2 B	5.3 C	5.4 A	5.5 A	5.6 C	5.7 A
5.8 D	5.9 B	5.10 D	5.11 A	5.12 A	5.13 D	5.14 A
5.15 A	5.16 A	5.17 A	5.18 B	5.19 B	5.20 A	5.21 A
5.22 A	5.23 B	5.24 B	5.25 A	5.26 A	5.27 B	5.28 A
5.29 D	5.30 A	5.31 A	5.32 A	5.33 D	5.34 A	5.35 A
5.36 D	5.37 D	5.38 A				

Chapter 6
HOW CAN YOU CREATE A SAFE, EFFICIENT, ACTIVITY-BASED SCIENCE CLASSROOM?
Test Items

THE FOLLOWING ARE **MULTIPLE CHOICE** QUESTIONS. Select the single best answer for each question.

6.1. - 6.5 The following statements refer to **science safety practices**. Indicate whether the statement is: **A = True B = False.**

6.1. Any time the students are doing an activity in the lab where there is even the slightest chance of something getting into an eye, goggles should be worn.

6.2. If a teacher discovers that something in the classroom does not meet safety standards, he/she should initiate correction, preferably in writing to administrators, as soon as possible.

6.3. If an activity is found in a science textbook it must already meet safety standards.

6.4. As long as a school sponsored field trip takes place during school hours you can take a child on the trip without getting signed parental release forms.

6.5. On field trips the buddy system should be implemented. This eliminates the need for additional adult supervisors.

6.6 - 6.16 The following statements refer to **science safety equipment**. Indicate whether the statement is: **A = True B = False.**

6.6. Extension cords should not be used to operate hot plates since a sufficient number of electrical outlets must be available in a safe science classroom.

6.7. Electrical outlet caps should be in place when outlets are not used in the presence of young children.

6.8. Electrical outlets within reach of a sink or faucet should be protected by a ground-fault circuit interrupting device.

6.9. If alcohol burners, sterno or candles are to used as a source of heat, they should be placed in pie pans of damp sand.

6.10. Adding a pinch of table salt to alcohol burner fuel helps to make the flame easier to see.

6.11. Any flammable liquids must be stored in an approved safety can made of heavy gauge steel or polyethylene with a spring loaded lid.

6.12. Loose clothing and hair must be restricted when children are working around open flames.

6.13. Fire blankets can be made of any type of material and of any convenient size.

6.14. Fire extinguishers should be located in close proximity to the classroom and children should instructed in their proper uses.

6.15. Eye washes and an emergency shower should be installed in permanent science labs. In an emergency, bottled water stations can be used as a temporary safety precaution.

6.16. Approved safety goggles display the rating of Z87.

6.17 - 6.21 Match the following safety concepts with the appropriate example by using the following codes:

A = **Tort**
B = **Reasonable and Prudent Judgment**
C = **Negligence**
D = **Due Care**
E = **Foreseeable Hazards**

6.17. What is Mr. Sludge trying to determine when he examines and tests the appropriateness of an activity before he actually does the activity in class with students?

6.18. Ms. Martinez is a teacher who files a request for a safety correction with the school administration. From a safe science perspective, what is she practicing?

6.19. ________ must be proven before a person can be held accountable for personal injury.

6.20. All teachers have a responsibility to exercise ________ while protecting the students in their charge.

6.21. A ______ is a wrong or an injury that is committed against someone else which may result in the injured party seeking restitution.

6.22. The storage of science equipment was the subject of a teacher lounge debate. Several argued in favor of keeping materials in their own classrooms. Which argument would best justify that position?

A) When I want to do a science activity I know the materials I need will be there because I'm the only one using them.
B) I identify my science materials needs early in the year so that I can get everything I need out of our budget. I don't see a need to share these with anyone.
C) I'll have more resources this way.
D) I don't want to have to rely on anyone else supplying me with science materials.
E) None of the above.

6.23. In a teacher lounge discussion the principal made the case for a central storage area for scientific equipment. Which argument do you think she employed to get the teachers to understand the value of a central storage area?

A) You won't have to spend a lot of your own money for science supplies.
B) You will have access to more equipment.
C) It's easier to keep track of materials in a central storage area.
D) There's less danger of students getting into equipment when stored in a central location.
E) More than one of these arguments.

6.24 - 6.30 Indicate whether each of the following is either true or false.
Use: **A = True and B = False**

6.24 Plastic storage bins with lids are considered indestructible and can hold more materials than traditional cardboard shoe boxes.

6.25. A recycling center is a good area to find materials for science projects.

6.26. A well designed science classroom will have a sink.

6.27. Classrooms with desks instead of tables can not be used to teach effective science lessons.

6.28. A science learning center can be used to conduct individual student research.

6.29. The research states that effective science instruction is not prohibited by class size.

6.30. In arranging an effective, efficient, safe, activity-based science classroom, the science curriculum should not dictate how the room is arranged.

CHAPTER 6
Answer Key for Test Items

6.1	A	6.2	A	6.3	B	6.4	B	6.5	B	6.6	A	6.7	A
6.8	A	6.9	A	6.10	A	6.11	A	6.12	A	6.13	B	6.14	A
6.15	A	6.16	A	6.17	E	6.18	B	6.19	C	6.20	D	6.21	A
6.22	A	6.23	B	6.24	B	6.25	A	6.26	A	6.27	B	6.28	A
6.29	B	6.30	B										

Chapter 7
WHAT ARE THE CHARACTERISTICS OF EFFECTIVE SCIENCE MATERIALS AND PROGRAMS?
Test Items

THE FOLLOWING ARE **MULTIPLE CHOICE** QUESTIONS. Select the single best answer for each question.

7.1. Science curriculum development has changed since the 1957 Sputnik launch. Which of the following curriculum development processes has significantly effected science education in today's schools?

A) Allowing science textbook publishers to determine which science series is the most successful, and then adopting that for a science program.
B) Looking at the science programs from several large school districts throughout the nation, look for similarities and differences, combining the best of all and then adopting that as the model science curriculum.
C) Teachers of like grade levels share *what works* for them. Best of each is combined to make the ideal science curriculum.
D) Experts in science pedagogy, science knowledge, and classroom teachers come together to share ideas on science concepts, methodologies, and processes which they believe are important for all school children to experience. From their work a science curriculum is developed.
E) None of the above have significantly brought about changes in science curriculum today.

7.2. Mr. Stevens, the fifth grade science teacher, sent a note to the parents explaining his science program. He stated that he expects his students to not only engage in many scientific explorations throughout the year, but that he also would like them to interview their parents about their career and to determine how concepts they're learning in science class are related to their parent's career. Mr. Stevens stated that he is encouraging his students to share with the class any newspaper or magazine articles they come across which deal with recent scientific achievements. As a class they will look at the impact of those achievements on society. Mr. Stevens is:

A) Encouraging interest in possible science related careers.
B) Getting students excited about science by doing the things scientists do rather than talking about them.
C) Helping the students understand how science is related to society.
D) Creating students who will have a more global view of science and its uses for the future.
E) All of the above.

7.3. The Three Big Elementary Science Curricula, ESS, SCIS, and SAPA:

A) Were more hands-on than descriptive.
B) Expected a change in the traditional teacher role.
C) Placed a greater emphasis on active learner participation.
D) Did not follow the typical collection of science content units of instruction that stressed reading and vocabulary development.
E) All of the above.

7.4. Which of the following does the SAPA program <u>NOT</u> endorse?

A) Science content should be systematically related to a particular science discipline.

B) Science content should be selected from familiar objects and phenomena in the child's world.
C) Science lessons should be arranged in an orderly, sequential manner.
D) Objectives should be described very specifically in terms of student behaviors.

7.5. How does ESS differ from other innovative science curriculum?
A) The activities are only for intermediate grades.
B) Getting teacher input for material development.
C) Providing material kits for exploration activities.
D) It is a collection of non-sequential units on various science topics.
E) Scientists were not used to help develop the units.

7.6. Science Curriculum Improvement Study was primarily designed to:
A) Provide children with numerous experiences using science process skills.
B) Allow children to explore science concepts before the concept is invented.
C) More accurately assess student attitudes and interests toward the science activities.
D) None of the above.
E) All of the above.

7.7. How have ESS, SCIS, and SAPA influenced today's elementary science programs?
A) Internationally, U.S. children's science achievement outranks the most advanced industrialized countries.
B) Today's elementary science textbooks are much improved and contain many features originally shown among these programs.
C) Most U. S. school districts have a hands-on science curriculum.
D) All elementary teachers use a discovery approach to science teaching.
E) More students choose to enroll in high school science courses and more pursue science related careers than ever before.

Items 7.8 - 7.13. The following are **TRUE or FALSE.** On your answer sheet, mark either letter **A = TRUE** or letter **E = FALSE.**

7.8. *Project Synthesis* is important because it identifies what should be included in elementary science programs.

7.9. *Project Synthesis* research reported by Ted Bredderman and Jim Shymansky verifies that hands-on science programs can produce advances in student learning beyond what is usually received from text based teacher-centered science programs.

7.10. Researchers urge school districts to abandon their text dominated science programs in favor of purchasing new non-text, hands-on, manipulative science programs.

7.11. The *Project Synthesis* research verifies that SAPA's structured learning approach results in the greatest increase in student attitudes toward science than ESS or SCIS.

7.12. SCIS produces greater process skill development among children than ESS or SAPA, according to *Project Synthesis* research.

7.13. Of the three, SCIS is more balanced and has produced measurably greater gains in pupil science achievement than ESS or SAPA.

Refer to the following figure for answering the following questions, 7.14 - 7.16. It is a continuum that can be used to locate the main elementary science projects, ESS, SAPA, and SCIS.

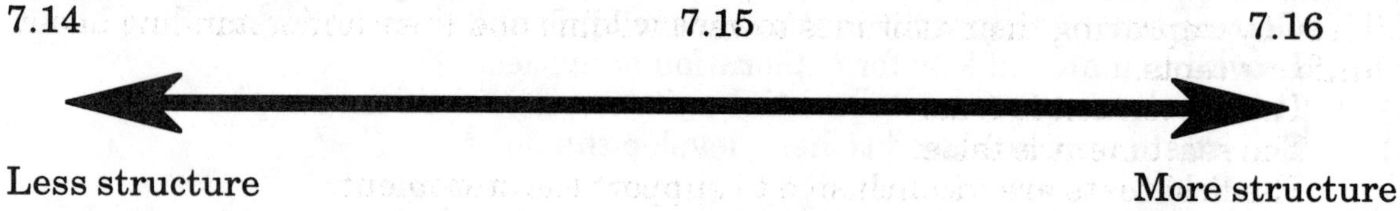

7.14. Which project is located here and is marked by unstructured units featuring a variety of science topics designed to emphasize attitudinal development?
A) The Elementary Science Study
B) Project Learning Tree
C) Science-A Process Approach
D) Science Curriculum Improvement Study
E) Outdoor Biology Instructional Strategies

7.15. Which project is located here and is known for its process and content balance, making the greatest gains in student achievement possible through the learning cycle.
A) The Elementary Science Study
B) Project Learning Tree
C) Science-A Process Approach
D) Science Curriculum Improvement Study
E) Project WILD

7.16. Which project is located here and is known for emphasis on behavioral objectives and sequential modules? There are 105 modules organized around the science processes where content is of lesser importance.
A) The Elementary Science Study
B) Project Learning Tree
C) Science-A Process Approach
D) Science Curriculum Improvement Study
E) Discrepant Events

7.17. " ... to assist learners of any age in developing awareness, knowledge, skills and commitment to result in informed decisions, responsible behavior, and constructive actions ...." is the goal of:
A) OBIS
B) Super Saver Investigator
C) Project WILD
D) SCIS
E) all of the above

7.18. " ...teach people how to think, not what to think" is a characteristic of:
A) OBIS
B) Project WILD
C) Project WILD Aquatic
D) Project Learning Tree
E) answers B, C

7.19. The field test research reveals that Project WILD makes a positive impact on children by improving their attitudes toward wildlife and their understanding about wildlife concepts.
A) The statement is true.
B) The statement is false.
C) The field tests are inconclusive to support the statement.

7.20. "Oh Deer!" is an important activity because it:
A) Teaches the interrelationships of components in a habitat.
B) Shows the variations in a population over time.
C) Emphasizes the dependence of a species on its habitat.
D) Illustrates what can happen to an animal population with uncontrolled hunting.
E) All of the above.

7.21. What is the single most important contribution of a curriculum supplement like Project WILD?
A) It restores fun to learning.
B) It provides an exceptionally thorough concept outline to add clarity and rigor to a curriculum.
C) It provides many new activities which are fun to do.
D) It helps to bring the study of wildlife inside.
E) It helps to protect animals like Bambi.

7.22. *Project Learning Tree* is:
A) An innovative science program geared toward the physical sciences.
B) A forestry lobbyist who works for public clients.
C) A science program emphasizing a process approach.
D) A hands-on curriculum supplement with an environmental emphasis on plant life.
E) An action-oriented supplemental program with an emphasis on the conserving environmental resources.

7.23. Project WILD *Aquatic* is a program that:
A) Is designed for grades 4 - 10.
B) Emphasizes learning biology outdoors.
C) Includes the study of plants and animals.
D) Provides concrete and creative experiences for children to learn about aquatic concepts in and out of doors.
E) All of the above.

7.24. Project *WILD* is:
A) Helpful in stimulating awareness and responsible human actions.
B) Emphasizes wildlife concepts.
C) Useful as a curriculum supplement.
D) All of the above.

E) B and C only.

7.25. The next generation of science programs were designed to meet the needs of:
A) All learners, not just the intellectually elite.
B) Classroom teachers with a greater background in science.
C) Only constructivist educators.
D) School districts with little to no budget for science supplies.
E) None of the above.

CHAPTER 7
Answer Key for Test Items

7.1	D	7.2	E	7.3	E	7.4	A	7.5	D	7.6	D	7.7	B
7.8	A	7.9	A	7.10	B	7.11	B	7.12	B	7.13	A	7.14	A
7.15	D	7.16	C	7.17	A	7.18	E	7.19	A	7.20	E	7.21	D
7.22	D	7.23	D	7.24	D	7.25	A						

Chapter 8
HOW CAN YOU IMPROVE YOUR SCIENCE INSTRUCTION THROUGH HUMAN, PRINT, AND MULTIMEDIA RESOURCES?

THE FOLLOWING ARE **MULTIPLE CHOICE** QUESTIONS. Select the single best answer for each question.

8.1. Which of the following is NOT a prime reason for using telecommunication networks?
A) Networks help overcome teacher isolation.
B) Children benefit from a break in the normal routine and network communications entertain them while they learn.
C) With supplementary teacher materials, networks can be utilized in the science curriculum.
D) Networks increase access to information.
E) Networks help to diffuse new ideas and resources rapidly.

8.2. The main purpose of an activity such as a nature walk is to:
A) Allow children to become more aware of the things in the natural world around them.
B) Stimulate and encourage inquiry.
C) Encourage children to make collections.
D) Discover the unexpected.
E) Take a break from classroom seat work.

8.3. Prior to a science field trip, it would be best to do which of the following?
A) Have a group of children who have carefully previewed a good film on the subject present it properly to the class.
B) Have a child who has been there before tell about what s/he saw.
C) Have the person in charge of the place to be visited talk to the class.
D) Have a group of children who have made some preparations discuss with the class the reason for the trip and what to look for.
E) Plan to be absent and let a substitute take care of the trip.

8.4. A very practical resource for elementary science teachers is:
A) A computer network link to NASA.
B) A fellow teacher.
C) Elementary students in higher grade levels.
D) Local adult volunteers.
E) All of the above.

8.5. The best reason to use outside resources for science teaching is:
A) Community resources can enhance student interest.
B) A real world link between science concepts can be made.
C) They increase the depth and breadth of the teaching/learning experience.
D) All of the above.
E) None of the above.

8.6. Which of the following is not a benefit provided through a school/business partnership?
A) They provide a bridge between business and industry with educators.
B) Businesses have greater input into the type of curriculum offered by schools.

C) They provide a vehicle for business and education to address the goal of a better educated citizenry.
D) Business can provide financial support through donations of money, computer software, or employee knowledge to share with students and staff.
E) All of the above are benefits.

8.7. Mr. Smith had three computers in his room that he let children work on after they finished their written assignments. Most often the children did drill and practice software until they got bored with it. Mr. Smith uses microcomputers in his class:
A) At the most basic level I.
B) To keep the children from getting into trouble.
C) To engage them in a deeper exploration of the subject matter.
D) To help his students to expand their understanding of a concept.
E) As a tool to help the students learn higher order thinking skills.

8.8. Mrs. Carlson heard about this research project her students could join in on over the internet by tracking the migration of butterflies. She already had her students using the computers to analyze data from previous experiments and thought this would be a great opportunity for her class. Which statement is most true about Mrs. Carlson's use of microcomputers?
A) Computers are used for nothing more than drill and practice, to learn a science fact.
B) Computers can assist in conceptualization.
C) Information can be easily accessed using a internet link.
D) Computers can be used to store data.
E) Computers can not be used to manipulate data.

8.9 If a teacher accesses lesson plans electronically, i.e. through a particular science group WEB site, then the information is accurate and truly engaging for the students.
A) Always
B) Almost Always
C) Not necessarily since almost anyone can enter information to some sites.
D) Never
E) You can't put lessons on WEB sites

Items 8.10 - 8.20. Indicate whether each of the following is true or false.
Use **A = True and B = False**

8.10. A Parental Permission for Out-of-classroom Activity Slip has to be signed by the parent or guardian for a child to participate in an out-of-school activity.

8.11. A field trip helps children to organize new information in relation to their experiences.

8.12. As a teacher your use of resources is only limited to your imagination and energy.

8.13. Computer communication networks provide support for rapid diffusion of innovative techniques and procedures among teachers.

8.14. Concrete experiences help students acquire and retain basic science skills.

8.15. A field trip provides a valuable correlation of subjects.

8.16. The link between the community and the classroom is not a new concept. John Dewey wrote about this idea in 1916.

8.17. Community volunteers do not need to receive some training and/or background information before they start to assist in the classroom.

8.18. It is smart practice to hear the guest speaker speak ahead of time to determine how well the speaker will interact with the students.

8.19. To determine if computer software should be used in your science class you should be able to identify the science concepts it teaches and determine how engaging it is for the student's intellect.

8.20. An advantage to using authoring software such as *Hyperstudio* is that you could design the kinds of experiences you want your students to have and make it as meaningful and engaging as you want it to be.

CHAPTER 8
Answer Key for Test Items

8.1	B	8.2	B	8.3	D	8.4	E	8.5	D	8.6	B	8.7	A
8.8	B	8.9	C	8.10	A	8.11	A	8.12	A	8.13	A	8.14	A
8.15	A	8.16	A	8.17	B	8.18	A	8.19	A	8.20	A		

Chapter 9
WHAT TEACHING METHODS HELP LEARNERS TO CONSTRUCT MEANING?
Test Items

THE FOLLOWING ARE **MULTIPLE CHOICE** QUESTIONS. Select the single best answer for each question.

9.1. During a hands-on science activity, Mr. Grover notices a group of students discussing the activity. They appear to be having a severe disagreement and ask for Mr. Grover to solve the problem. As the teacher, what should he do if he prefers to create and maintain a successful atmosphere of cooperative learning?
A) Point out that the Principal Investigator is in charge of group management, then walk away and let the PI do her or his job.
B) Ask the Maintenance Director to clean up and put the group on notice that they are to be quiet the rest of the class period.
C) As the Recorder to state the group's findings so far, then tell the group what to do in order to finish the activity correctly.
D) Tell the group the let the Reporter decide the disagreement since he (or she) will have to report the group's results to the entire class later.
E) Clarify any misunderstanding the group members may have about their roles and suggest that they cooperate with the rest of the individuals to arrive at a group conclusion.

9.2. What is a learning cycle?
A) A planning and teaching approach that is devoted only to science
B) A procedure for curriculum development and planning lessons
C) A way to teach and learn
D) All of the above
E) Answers B and C only

9.3. What is important about a learning cycle?
A) It influences how a teacher teaches and what children learn.
B) It contributes to superior pupil achievement when compared to the effects of the "inform-verify-practice" method of traditional texts.
C) It is consistent with how children learn in that "exploration" stimulates learner disequilibrium and fosters assimilation, whereas "conceptual invention" provides for learner accommodation and "expansion of the idea" helps learners to mentally organize.
D) All of the above
E) Answers A and C only

9.4. Ms. Rubella's cooperative science class was preparing to engage in a circuit activity. They had their bulbs, dry cells, and wires in hand. One student in group A noticed that their wires were totally covered with insulation so he got up and collected wire strippers for all the students in his work group. In Ms. Rubella's room what cooperative role do you think this student is serving?
A) Materials manger
B) Maintenance supervisor
C) Project director
D) Record keeper
E) Reporter

9.5 - 9.13 Indicate whether each of the following is either true or false about <u>discovery</u> or <u>inquiry</u> learning.
Use: **A = TRUE** and **B = FALSE.**

9.5. Inquiry is a process which can help children learn how to learn.

9.6. Inquiry teaching approaches seek to improve children's achievement levels, process skills and scientific attitudes.

9.7. A discovery is what a learner constructs in his or her mind.

9.8. Discovery is an outcome of an inquiry process.

9.9. Learning through inquiry suppresses the self-confidence levels of children.

9.10. Richard Suchman's inquiry method is based on convergent questions asked by teachers.

9.11. Suchman's inquiry method is centered around a discrepant event.

9.12. Suchman's inquiry method is designed to help students construct explanations for the natural phenomena that surrounds them.

9.13. The scientific teaching method emphasizes concepts and helps to improve student comprehension and retention.

9.14 - 9.39 The following questions are True or False and pertain to the Science Learning Cycle. Use: **A = TRUE** and **B = False**

9.14. The science learning cycle is **simply** a different way to plan lessons.

9.15. The science learning cycle is a planning, teaching, and learning method.

9.16. The science learning cycle is based on methods which are consistent with how children think, act, and learn.

9.17. The learning cycle is more than 20 years old and is based on Piagetian and concept development learning theory.

9.18. The learning cycle is a proven planning and teaching method as is evident in the extensive research conducted by science educators.

9.19. The single most critical aspect of a learning cycle is selecting a clear concept around which to structure the lesson.

9.20. The evaluation phase of the a learning may consist of pre-stated pupil performance objective or expected pupil outcomes for determining student learning.

9.21. The evaluation phase of the learning cycle must be done last to determine what students have learned.

9.22 - 9.25 Refer to the **EXPLORATION** phase of a science learning cycle.

9.22. Abstract concepts are developmentally inappropriate for elementary-aged children; appropriate hands-on materials with a learning cycle helps to make the concepts more concrete and more developmentally suited to young children.

9.23. The Exploration phase is teacher-centered and states the concept.

9.24. Instructions must be given which introduce the children to the materials, the materials must represent the concept, but the instructions must not name or tell the concept.

9.25. The purpose of the exploration phase is to explain the purpose of the lesson.

9.26 - 9.32 Refer to the **EXPLANATION** phase of a science learning cycle.

9.26. The explanation phase functions as a way to create learner disequilibrium.

9.27. The explanation phase encourage learner accommodation.

9.28. The teacher must carefully set the environment, which may be teacher-centered.

9.29. The teacher's primary role is to collect the information the children have uncovered during the exploration and use it with the rest of the class to "invent" the concept.

9.30. The teacher must guide the students as they "invent" the concept.

9.31. The concept must be made concrete, and is best if written on the chalkboard with special attention called to it.

9.32. In the explanation phase, a teacher's mission is to help students construct the concept which represents the main idea of the lesson.

9.33 - 9.39 Refer to the **EXPANSION** phase of a science learning cycle.

9.33. New concepts must be linked to previously learned ideas or learner experiences.

9.34. The teacher's purpose in this mostly student-centered phase is to expand the students' thinking beyond their present experiences and thinking limits.

9.35. The dimensions around which the goals for science education cluster around easily fit into the philosophy of the Expansion phase because these dimensions intend to expand the student's perceptions of science's values and uses.

9.36. The purpose of the Expansion phase is to help students organize their thinking by relating it to what they have just learned in the concept invention phase.

9.37. The language of the concept must be used by the students during the Expansion phase for students to experience the full power of the cycle and to receive its full benefits.

9.38. The expansion phase permits a teacher to use additional activities to help learners add depth to their concept formation.

9.39. The expansion phase provides an effective method for addressing the four dimensions of science goals.

CHAPTER 9
Answer Key for Test Items

9.1	E	9.2	C	9.3	D	9.4	A	9.5	A	9.6	AB	9.7	B
9.8	A	9.9	B	9.10	B	9.11	A	9.12	A	9.13	A	9.14	B
9.15	A	9.16	A	9.17	A	9.18	A	9.19	A	9.20	A	9.21	B
9.22	A	9.23	B	9.24	A	9.25	B	9.26	B	9.27	A	9.28	A
9.29	A	9.30	A	9.31	A	9.32	A	9.33	A	9.34	A	9.35	A
9.36	A	9.37	A	9.38	A	9.39	A						

Chapter 10
WHAT DO YOU NEED TO KNOW ABOUT USING QUESTIONS AS A SCIENCE TEACHING TOOL?
Test Items

THE FOLLOWING ARE **MULTIPLE CHOICE** QUESTIONS. Select the single best answer for each question.

10.1. A teacher may help students to become good listeners if s/he:
- A) Asks "trick" questions on tests that cover some obscure point mentioned in class.
- B) Has the students repeat what was said by others in class.
- C) Focuses on the student and what he/she is saying, and give nonverbal cues to show that you are concerned that the rest of the class is listening.
- D) Uses the chalkboard or overhead projector to show an outline of the important topics to be discussed during the lesson.
- E) Gives occasional "pop" quizzes to make the students listen.

10.2. Which of the following suggestions provide keys to effective questioning?
- A) Plan specific questions and then use them to shape children's thinking in the direction desired.
- B) Ask your question before selecting a child to answer it.
- C) Talk less and ask more questions to encourage more student thinking and participation.
- D) Ask a variety of question types to encourage all children and to stimulate different level of thought.
- E) All of the above should be used as keys to effective questioning.

10.3. In formulating questions, it is most important to:
- A) Never include spontaneous questions.
- B) Be aware of your purpose so that you may construct and use the proper type of questions.
- C) Only ask questions during the exploration and expansion phase of the lesson.
- D) Avoid using children's questions.
- E) Avoid using evaluation questions for children in the primary grades.

10.4. Which of the following questions would most likely elicit convergent answers from students?
- A) How can we find out if heat affects dissolving time?
- B) What causes molecules of a liquid to move?
- C) How do your hands feel when you press them together and rapidly rub them?
- D) What do you think will happen when the mystery powder is heated?

10.5. A teacher who understands the value of well developed questions will probably never ask which of the following questions?
- A) How is sedimentary rock different from igneous?
- B) What do you think I might find inside of this geode?
- C) How could we find out if this crack in the rock is a fault line or simply a crack?
- D) Don't you see how the rocks are all green in color?
- E) Why should I wear safety goggles when I crack this rock?

10.6. Dr. Mary Budd Rowe's research on the effects of wait-time after a question is asked showed that:

A) The average wait-time allowed by most teachers was between 5 and 10 seconds.
B) When teachers increased wait-time, the students became frustrated and created discipline and management problems.
C) When teachers decreased the wait-time the students were able to give more answers.
D) When teachers increased wait-time, the quality and quantity of student responses increased significantly.

10.7. Open questions are high level questions and result in this type of thinking:

A) Cognitive memory
B) Convergent
C) Divergent
D) Social
E) None of the above

10.8. When a three second response time was given, Dr. Mary Budd Rowe discovered that discipline problems:

A) Decreased
B) Increased
C) Stayed the same
D) None of the above

10.9 In a traditional classroom setting, an inverted *T* shape is formed by teachers who ask children to respond. Which row is included every time?

A) Front
B) Middle
C) Second
D) Last
E) Side rows

10.10 Higher order thinking skills can be enhanced by asking questions such as:

A) What is the process whereby plants make their own food called?
B) How many observations did you make and record during your experiment?
C) What do you think caused the volcano to erupt?
D) Where can I find the island of Bimini on the map?
E) Can you use that data you collected and apply it to another area of research?

10.11 Closed questions are low level questions and result in this type of thinking:

A) Divergent
B) Evaluative
C) Convergent
D) Social
E) None of the above

10.12 - 10.20 The following are MATCHING items related to question categories. Match the question category to a question. Record:

A = Cognitive Memory **B = Evaluative Thinking**
C = Convergent Thinking **D = Divergent Thinking**

10.12. What is the average number of tornadoes for the month of April in this state?

10.13. How do you think the balls are similar?

10.14. How do you feel about working with the graphing calculator?

10.15. Is there a difference in height of the two basketball players?

10.16. What do you think causes the water to boil without the paper pan catching on fire?

10.17. What do you think will happen if these two chemicals are mixed?

10.18. What are the three states of matter?

10.19. What is your reason for stating that the Danube River is more polluted than the Mississippi River?

10.20. What was the purpose of adding the acid to the base solution?

CHAPTER 10
Answer Key for Test Items

10.1 C	10.2 E	10.3 B	10.4 B	10.5 D	10.6 D	10.7 C
10.8 D	10.9 C	10.10 E	10.11 C	10.12 A	10.13 D	10.14 B
10.15 A	10.16 D	10.17 D	10.18 A	10.19 B	10.20 C	

Chapter 11
HOW CAN YOU USE SCIENCE DEMONSTRATIONS AND TEXTBOOKS EFFECTIVELY?
Test Items

THE FOLLOWING ARE **MULTIPLE CHOICE** QUESTIONS. Select the single best answer for each question.

11.1. As an expository teacher the behavior Mrs. Smith exhibited was which of the following?
- A) Providing her students with background information Mrs. Smith proceeded to explain how photosynthesis worked.
- B) Mrs. Smith got a balloon and a knitting needle and thrust the needle into the balloon without popping it.
- C) Mrs. Smith divided the class into work groups, discussed the assignment and then began working with the student groups as they worked through the activity.
- D) Mrs. Smith's class planned in teams their next experiment and then suggested to her how they might go about acting on their plan.
- E) Mrs. Smith planned an experiment for her students before they named the concept.

11.2. Which of the following is not a true statement about choosing a textbook?
- A) Avoid texts that show science as absolute and unchanging.
- B) No single text can cover all viewpoints about a subject, but each should include acceptable alternatives.
- C) Bland textbooks, those written to avoid controversy are the best choice.
- D) Science portrayed retrospectively will not deal with current areas of research and problems.
- E) Beware of a textbook that does not represent the nature of science.

11.3. According to your text essential to a guided discovery lesson is:
- A) Closely following the written lesson plan.
- B) Asking well planned questions which allow for greater student participation.
- C) Involving children in the science processes.
- D) Making sure the students understand the concept.

11.4. A teaching demonstration typically is used to:
- A) Avoid placing children in danger.
- B) Over come equipment shortages.
- C) Arouse student interest and to raise important inquiry questions.
- D) Apply what has been studied by expanding student experiences.
- E) All of the above.

11.5. A principal believes in allowing each student to develop to his/her fullest potential. That principal may do which of the following as the BEST OPTION?
- A) Encourage Mr. Wickline to only use the textbook to plan and present lessons.
- B) Expect Mr. Wickline to use a text series different than those used by other teachers in the same school district, that is designed to stimulate learners.
- C) Suggest that Mr. Wickline take his class on numerous field trips throughout the school year.

D) Advise Mr. Wickline to visit other classes where the teacher has the children engaged in process oriented learning.

E) Demand that Mr. Wickline retire or risk being fired for incompetence.

11.6 - 11.20 The following are examples of "concepts" that may appear in science textbooks. It is important to select texts that are clear and accurate. Which are the BEST EXAMPLES of the clearest concepts?
Use **A = Agree** and **D = Disagree** for identifying the <u>best concepts</u>.

11.6. Students will identify the odors of foods.

11.7. Air currents are caused by the mixing of cold and warm air.

11.8. Using senses to identify animals.

11.9. Surface tension is when the water's surface acts as if it were covered with a thin skin.

11.10. Human skin cells are called epithelial cells and have some similarities to plant cells.

11.11. The children shall construct two types of circuits: open and closed.

11.12. The inner planets of the solar system are smaller and warmer than the outer planets.

11.13. Moving air pushes objects, and air slows moving objects.

11.14. Water has weight and helps things float.

11.15. Buoyancy is the name given to the upward force a liquid exerts on an object. If the upward force of the liquid is greater than the downward force of the object, the object will float.

11.16. Students will construct a list of metals and non-metals.

11.17. A "producer" makes food and contributes energy to a life cycle.

11.18. A "consumer" takes the food of a producer and uses it to its own advantage, contributing little to the energy flow of a life cycle.

11.19. A "decomposer" thrives on dead and decaying producers and consumers, breaking down matter into its most basic raw materials which can re-enter a life cycle.

11.20. Students will learn about electricity.

CHAPTER 11
Answer Key for Test Items

11.1 A	11.2 C	11.3 B	11.4 E	11.5 D	11.6 D	11.7 A
11.8 D	11.9 A	11.10 A	11.11 D	11.12 A	11.13 A	11.14 A
11.15 A	11.16 D	11.17 A	11.18 A	11.19 A	11.20 D	

Chapter
CONCEPT MAPS

CHAPTER 1

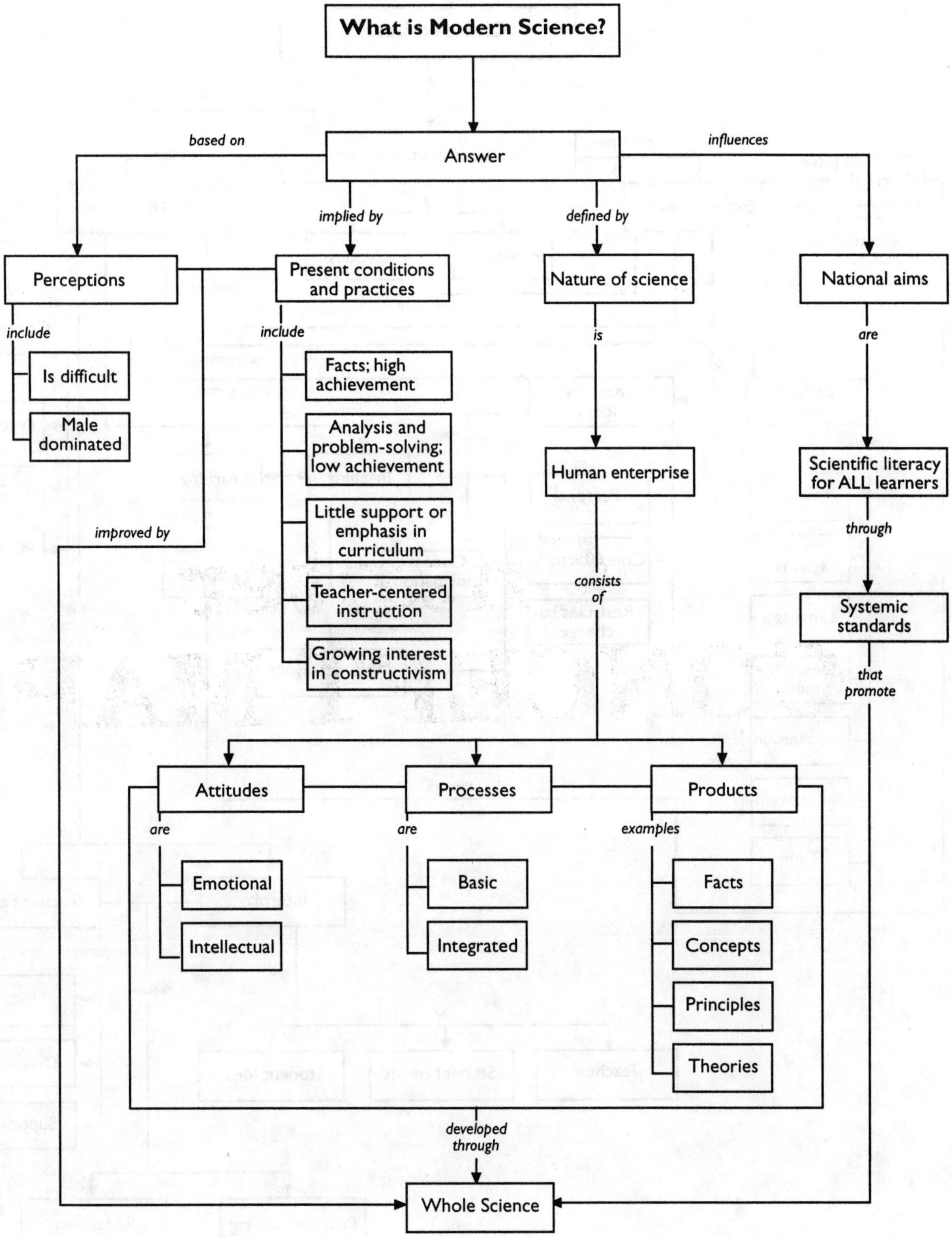

What is Modern Science?
Answer
based on
implied by
defined by
influences
Perceptions
Present conditions and practices
Nature of science
National aims
include
include
is
are
Is difficult
Male dominated
Facts; high achievement
Analysis and problem-solving; low achievement
Little support or emphasis in curriculum
Teacher-centered instruction
Growing interest in constructivism
Human enterprise
Scientific literacy for ALL learners
improved by
through
consists of
Systemic standards
that promote
Attitudes
Processes
Products
are
are
examples
Emotional
Intellectual
Basic
Integrated
Facts
Concepts
Principles
Theories
developed through
Whole Science

CHAPTER 2

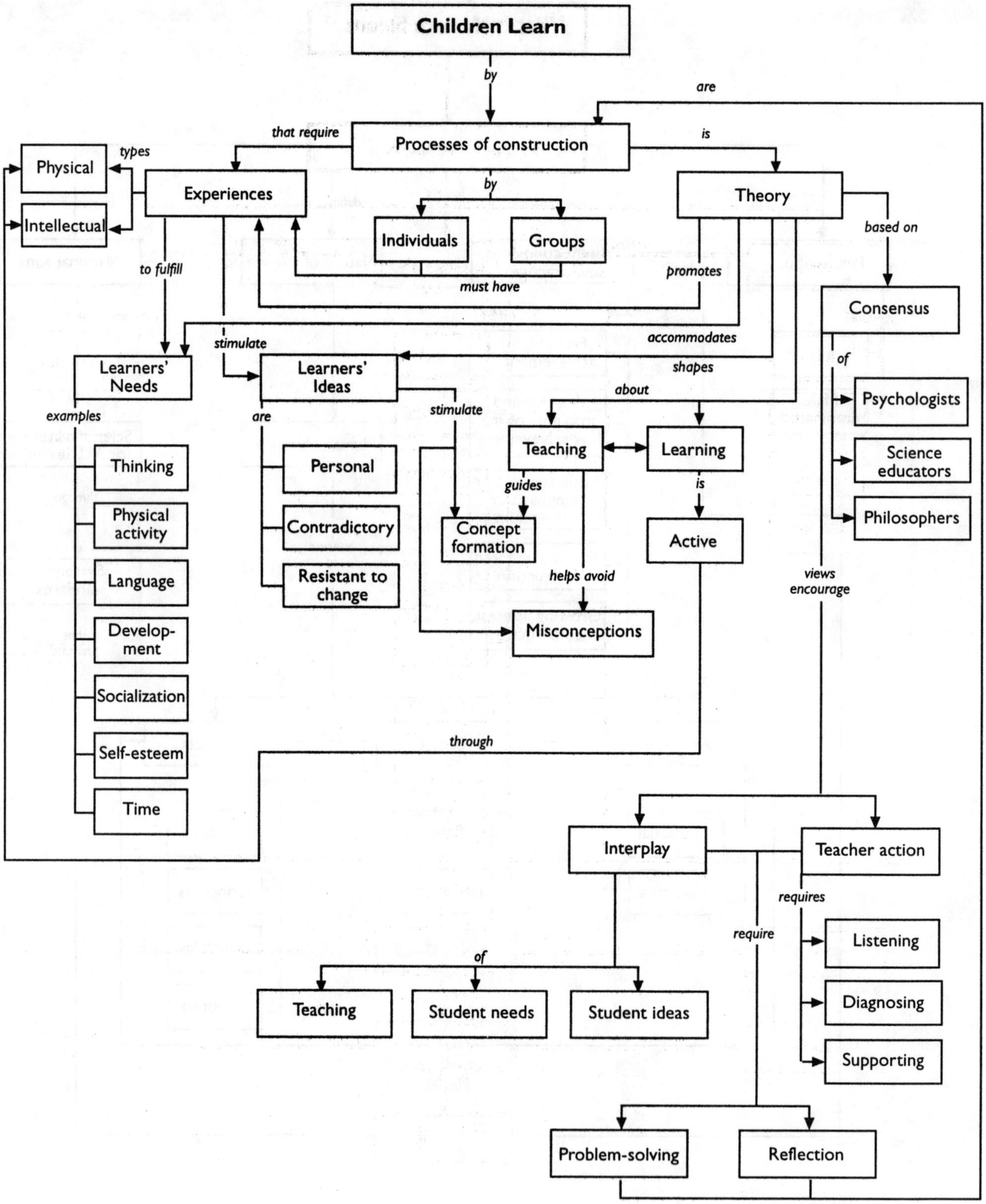

Children Learn
by
Processes of construction
that require
Experiences
types
Physical
Intellectual
by
Individuals
Groups
must have
is
are
Theory
based on
Consensus
of
Psychologists
Science educators
Philosophers
promotes
accommodates
shapes
about
to fulfill
Learners' Needs
examples
Thinking
Physical activity
Language
Develop-ment
Socialization
Self-esteem
Time
stimulate
Learners' Ideas
are
Personal
Contradictory
Resistant to change
stimulate
Teaching
Learning
guides
Concept formation
helps avoid
Misconceptions
is
Active
through
views encourage
Interplay
of
Teaching
Student needs
Student ideas
Teacher action
requires
Listening
Diagnosing
Supporting
require
Problem-solving
Reflection

CHAPTER 3

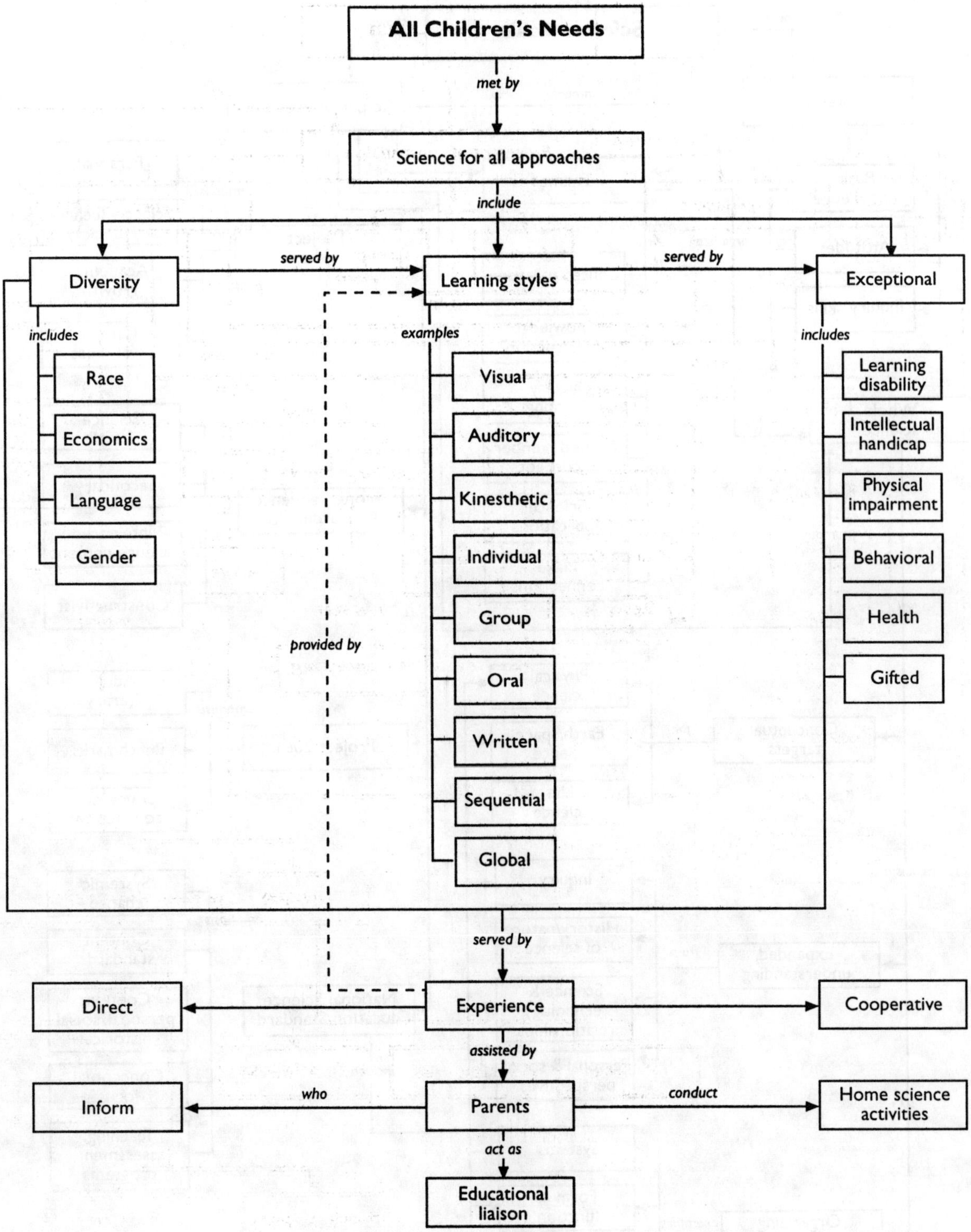
All Children's Needs
met by
Science for all approaches
include
Diversity
served by
Learning styles
served by
Exceptional
includes
Race
Economics
Language
Gender
examples
Visual
Auditory
Kinesthetic
Individual
Group
Oral
Written
Sequential
Global
includes
Learning disability
Intellectual handicap
Physical impairment
Behavioral
Health
Gifted
provided by
served by
Direct
Experience
Cooperative
assisted by
Inform
who
Parents
conduct
Home science activities
act as
Educational liaison

CHAPTER 4

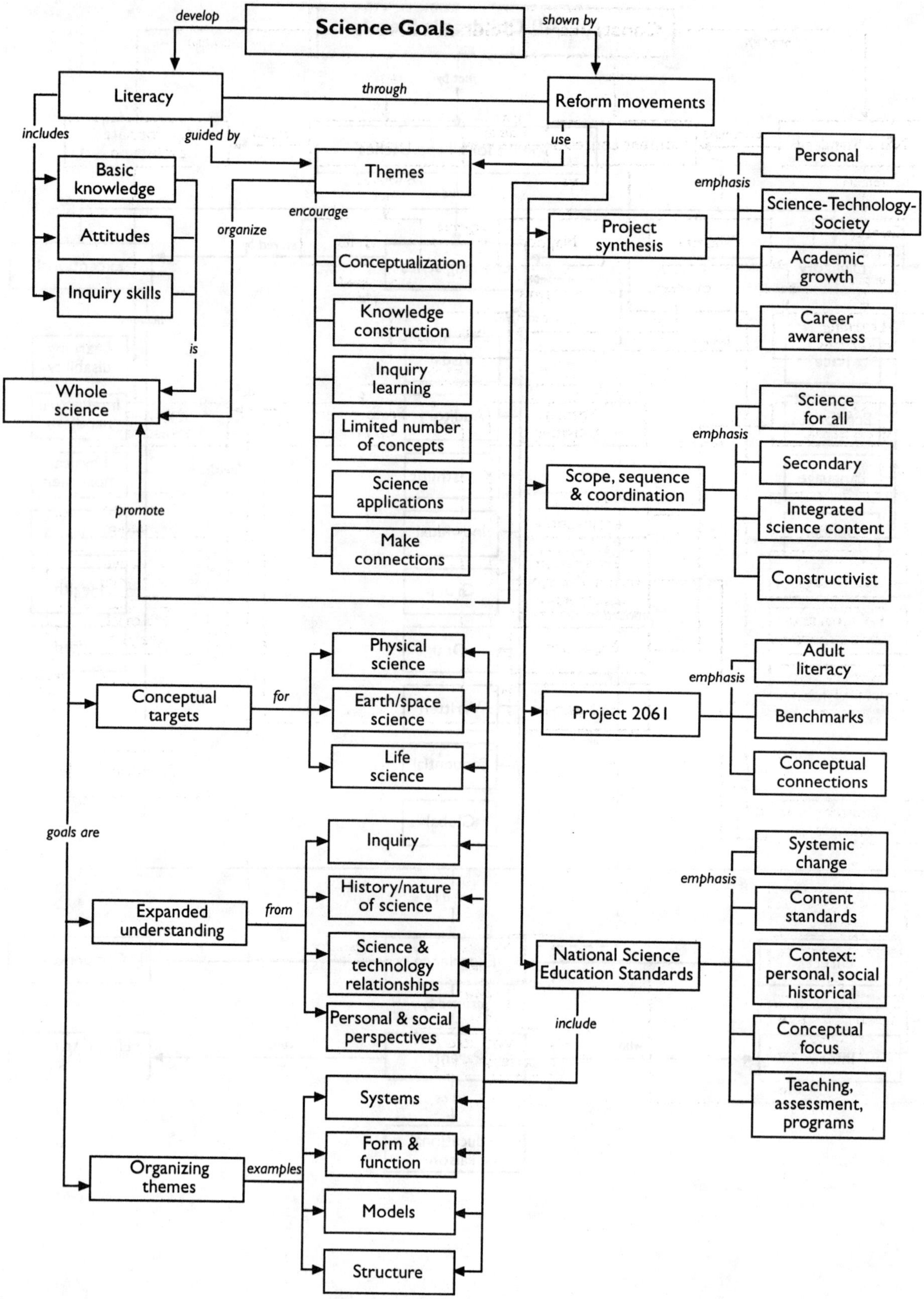
Science Goals
develop
shown by
Literacy
through
Reform movements
includes
guided by
use
Themes
Basic knowledge
Attitudes
Inquiry skills
organize
encourage
is
Whole science
Conceptualization
Knowledge construction
Inquiry learning
Limited number of concepts
Science applications
Make connections
promote
Project synthesis
emphasis
Personal
Science-Technology-Society
Academic growth
Career awareness
Scope, sequence & coordination
emphasis
Science for all
Secondary
Integrated science content
Constructivist
Conceptual targets
for
Physical science
Earth/space science
Life science
Project 2061
emphasis
Adult literacy
Benchmarks
Conceptual connections
goals are
Expanded understanding
from
Inquiry
History/nature of science
Science & technology relationships
Personal & social perspectives
National Science Education Standards
emphasis
Systemic change
Content standards
Context: personal, social historical
Conceptual focus
Teaching, assessment, programs
include
Organizing themes
examples
Systems
Form & function
Models
Structure

CHAPTER 5

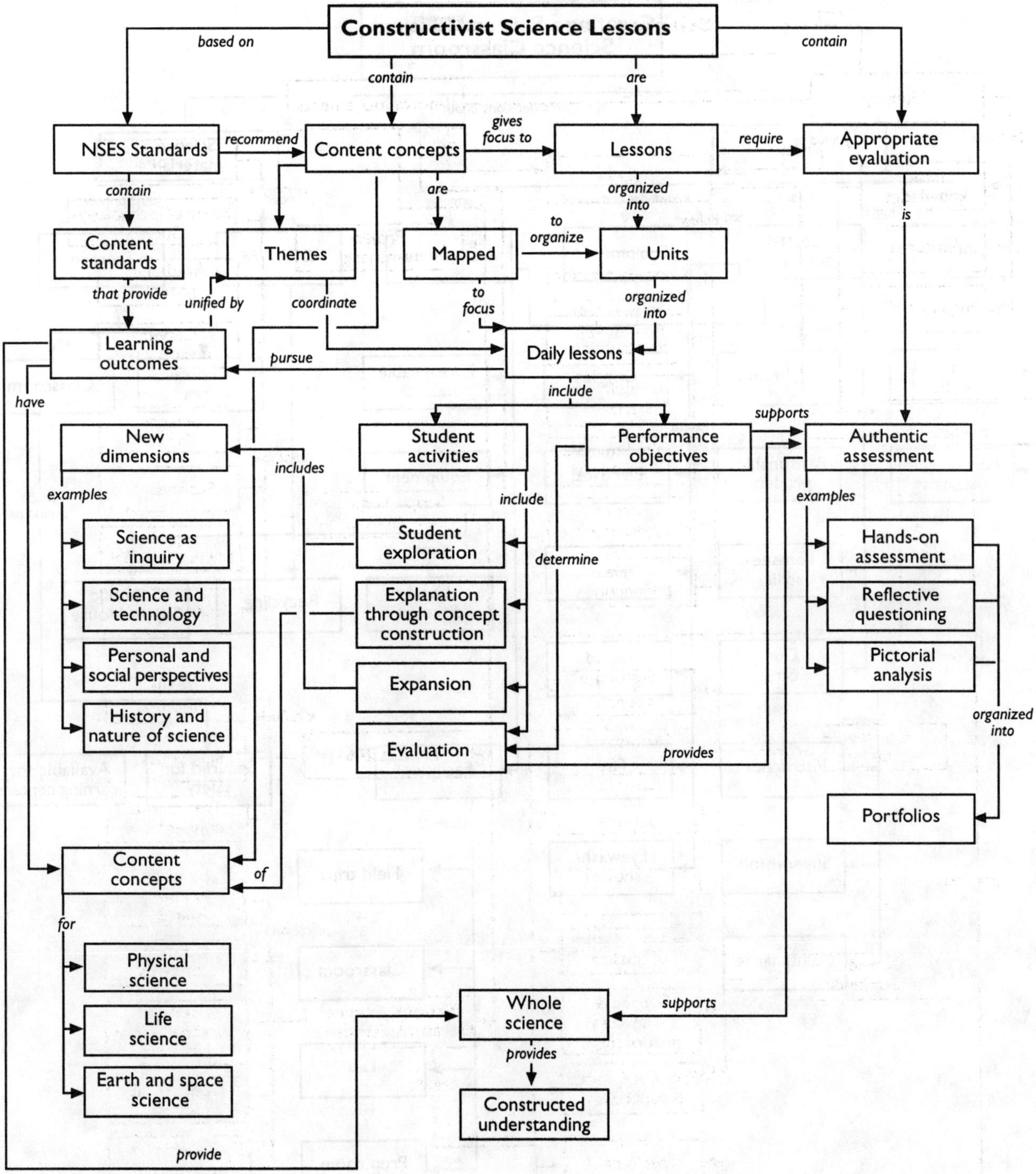

Constructivist Science Lessons
based on
contain
are
contain
NSES Standards
recommend
Content concepts
gives focus to
Lessons
require
Appropriate evaluation
contain
are
organized into
is
Content standards
Themes
Mapped
to organize
Units
that provide
unified by
coordinate
to focus
organized into
Learning outcomes
pursue
Daily lessons
have
include
supports
New dimensions
includes
Student activities
Performance objectives
Authentic assessment
examples
include
examples
Science as inquiry
Student exploration
determine
Hands-on assessment
Science and technology
Explanation through concept construction
Reflective questioning
Personal and social perspectives
Expansion
Pictorial analysis
History and nature of science
organized into
Evaluation
provides
Portfolios
Content concepts
of
for
Physical science
Life science
Whole science
supports
provides
Earth and space science
Constructed understanding
provide

CHAPTER 6

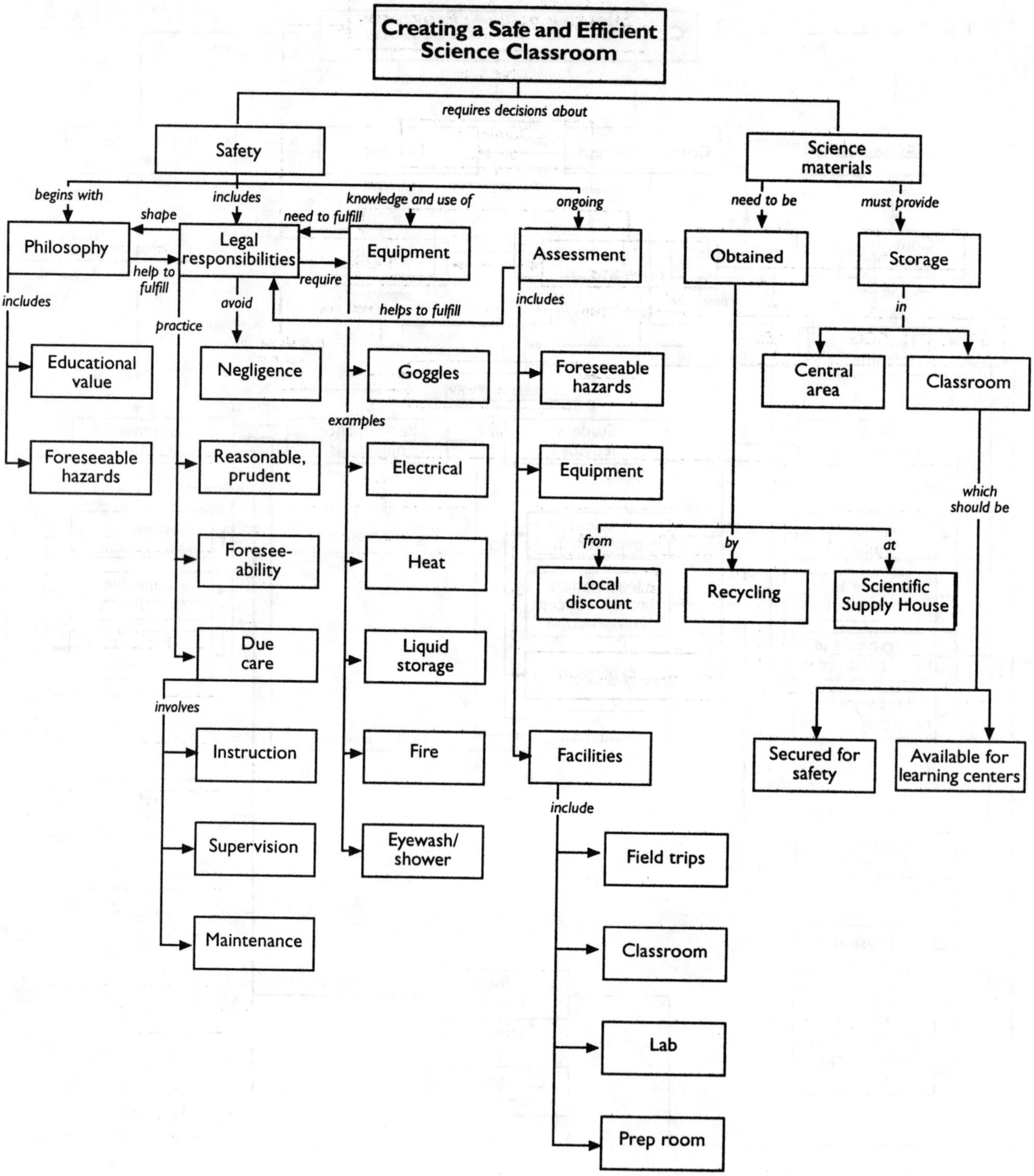
Creating a Safe and Efficient Science Classroom
requires decisions about
Safety
Science materials
begins with
includes
knowledge and use of
ongoing
need to be
must provide
shape
need to fulfill
Philosophy
Legal responsibilities
Equipment
Assessment
Obtained
Storage
help to fulfill
require
includes
avoid
helps to fulfill
includes
in
practice
Educational value
Negligence
Goggles
Foreseeable hazards
Central area
Classroom
examples
Foreseeable hazards
Reasonable, prudent
Electrical
Equipment
which should be
from
by
at
Foresee-ability
Heat
Local discount
Recycling
Scientific Supply House
Due care
Liquid storage
involves
Instruction
Fire
Facilities
Secured for safety
Available for learning centers
include
Supervision
Eyewash/ shower
Field trips
Maintenance
Classroom
Lab
Prep room

CHAPTER 7

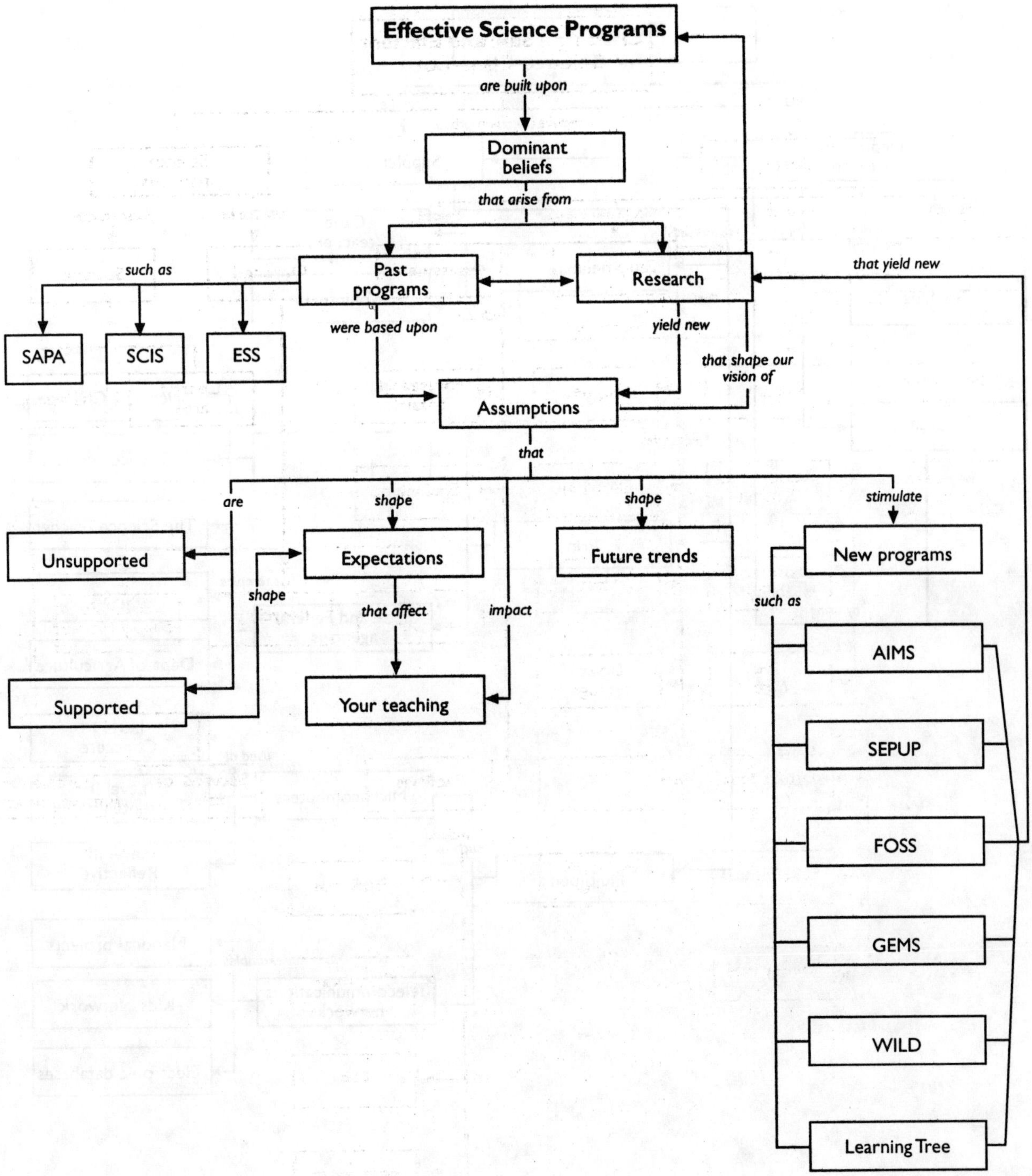
Effective Science Programs
are built upon
Dominant beliefs
that arise from
Past programs
Research
such as
SAPA
SCIS
ESS
were based upon
yield new
that shape our vision of
that yield new
Assumptions
that
are
shape
shape
stimulate
Unsupported
Expectations
Future trends
New programs
shape
that affect
impact
such as
Supported
Your teaching
AIMS
SEPUP
FOSS
GEMS
WILD
Learning Tree

CHAPTER 8

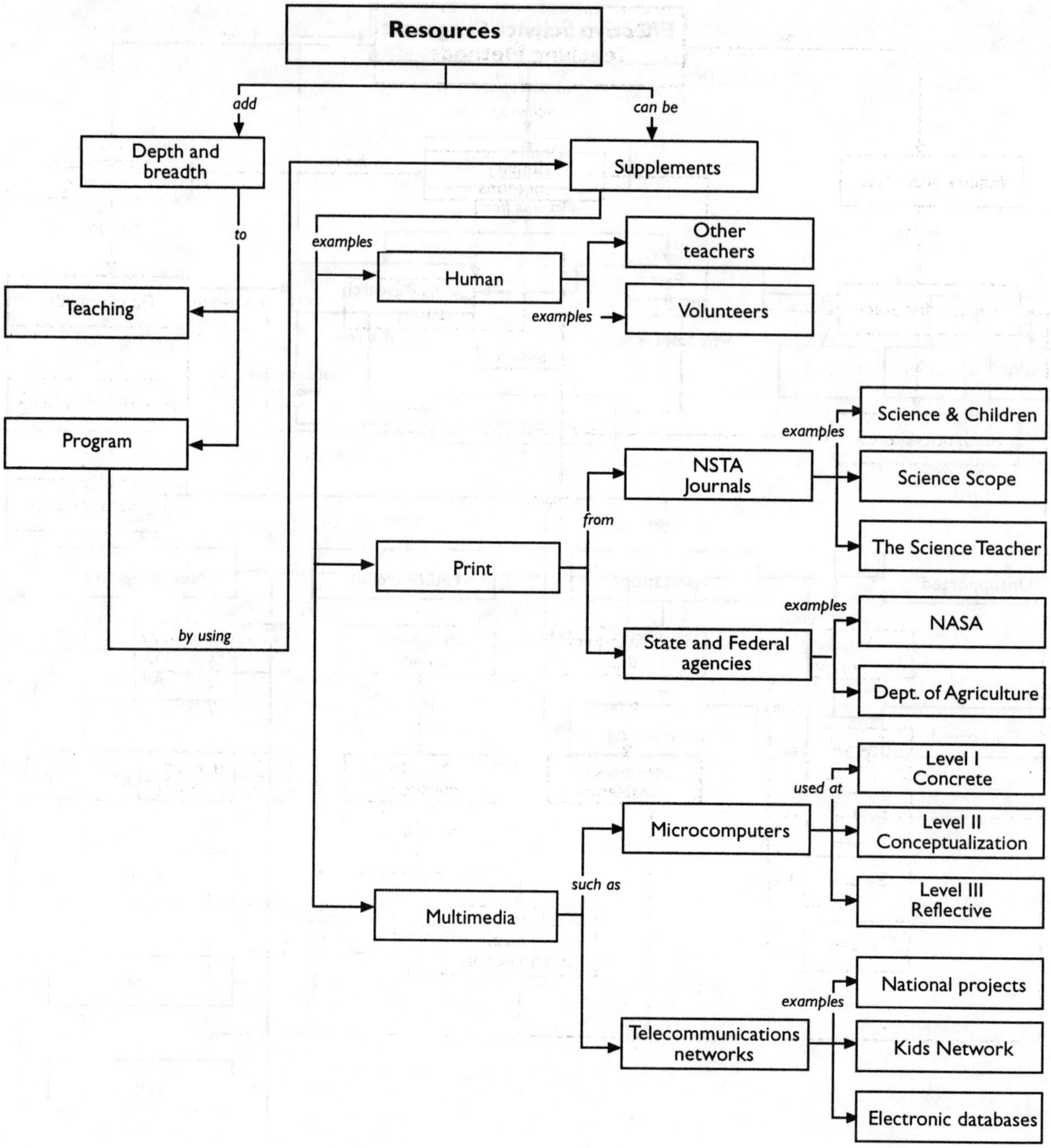

Resources
add
can be
Depth and breadth
to
Teaching
Program
by using
Supplements
examples
Human
Other teachers
Volunteers
Print
from
NSTA Journals
Science & Children
Science Scope
The Science Teacher
State and Federal agencies
NASA
Dept. of Agriculture
Multimedia
such as
Microcomputers
used at
Level I Concrete
Level II Conceptualization
Level III Reflective
Telecommunications networks
National projects
Kids Network
Electronic databases

CHAPTER 9

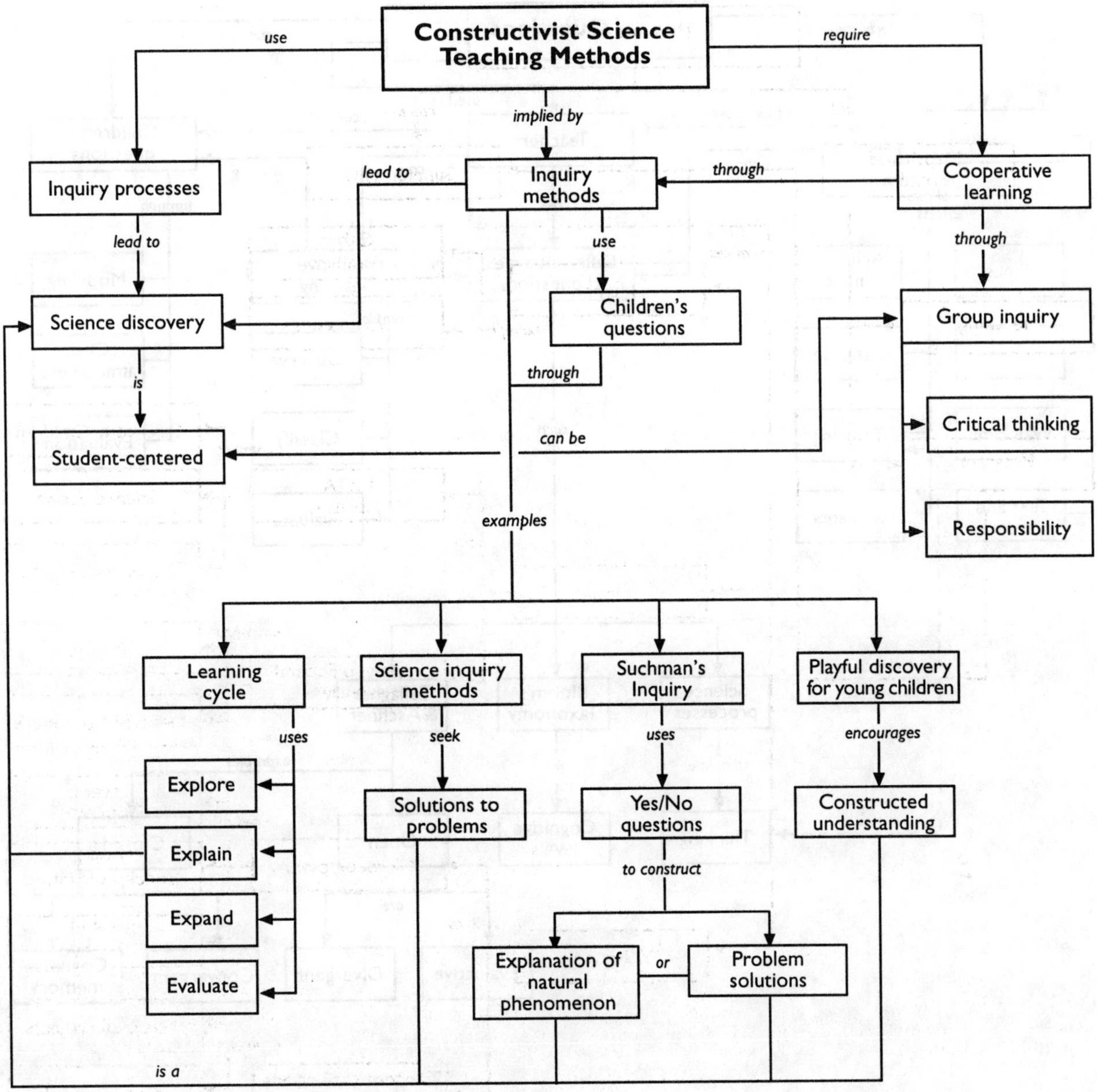

Constructivist Science Teaching Methods
use
require
implied by
Inquiry processes
lead to
Inquiry methods
through
Cooperative learning
lead to
use
through
Science discovery
Children's questions
Group inquiry
is
through
Critical thinking
Student-centered
can be
Responsibility
examples
Learning cycle
Science inquiry methods
Suchman's Inquiry
Playful discovery for young children
uses
seek
uses
encourages
Explore
Solutions to problems
Yes/No questions
Constructed understanding
Explain
to construct
Expand
Explanation of natural phenomenon
or
Problem solutions
Evaluate
is a

CHAPTER 10

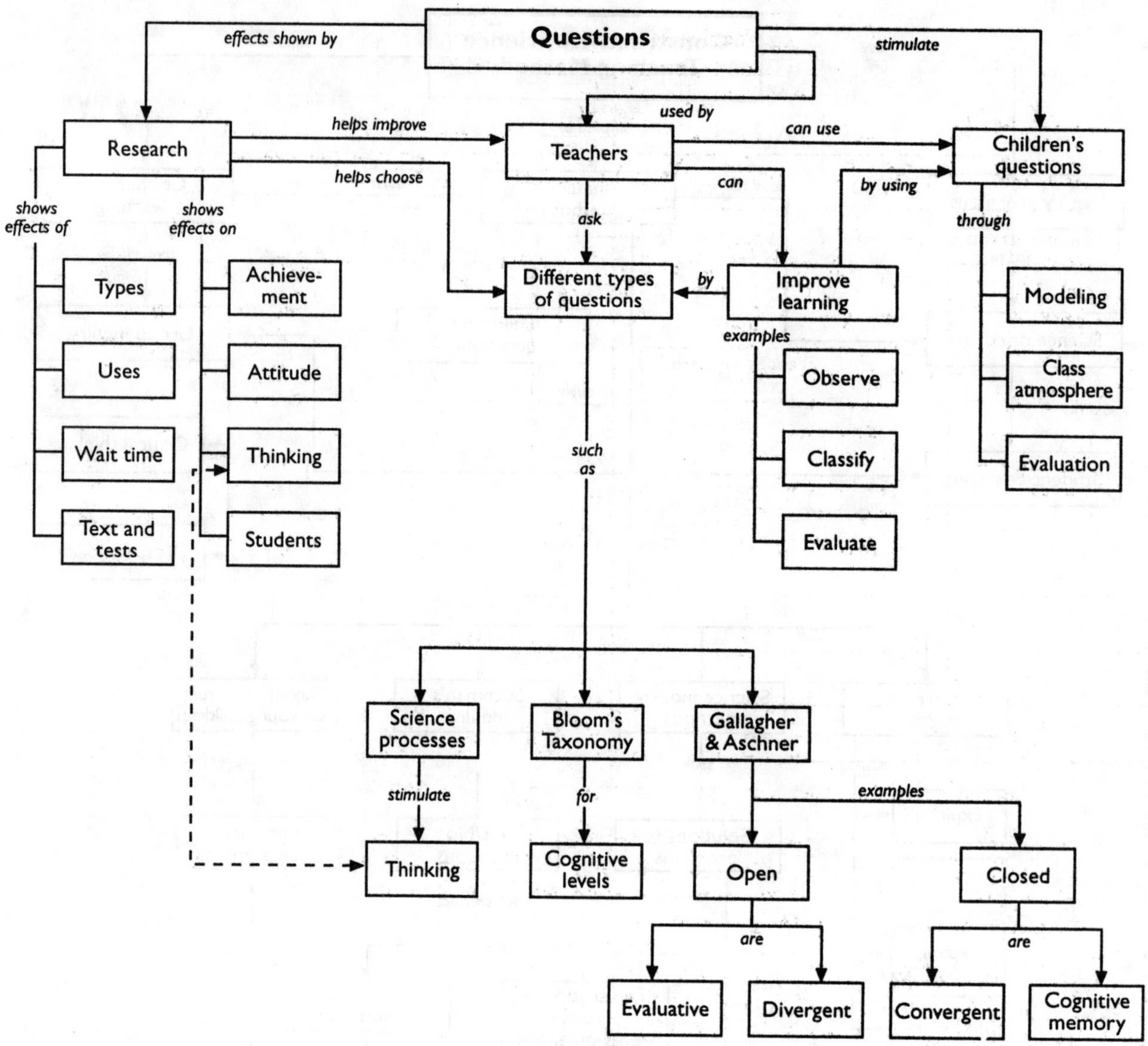
Questions
effects shown by
stimulate
used by
Research
helps improve
helps choose
Teachers
can use
can
Children's questions
by using
through
shows effects of
shows effects on
ask
Types
Uses
Wait time
Text and tests
Achievement
Attitude
Thinking
Students
Different types of questions
by
Improve learning
examples
Observe
Classify
Evaluate
Modeling
Class atmosphere
Evaluation
such as
Science processes
Bloom's Taxonomy
Gallagher & Aschner
stimulate
for
examples
Thinking
Cognitive levels
Open
Closed
are
are
Evaluative
Divergent
Convergent
Cognitive memory

CHAPTER 11

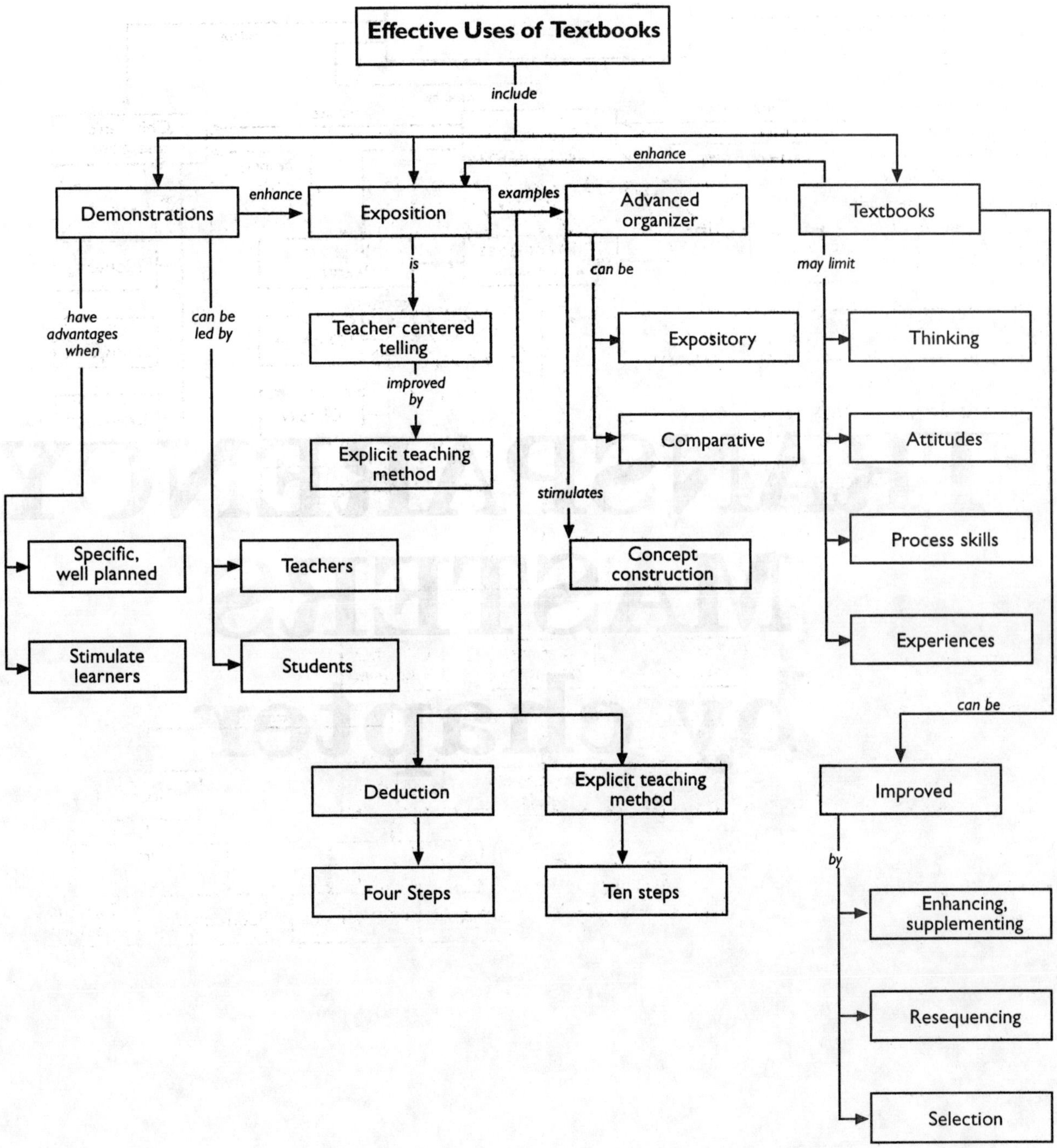
Effective Uses of Textbooks
include
Demonstrations
enhance
Exposition
examples
Advanced organizer
enhance
Textbooks
have advantages when
can be led by
is
can be
may limit
Teacher centered telling
improved by
Explicit teaching method
Expository
Comparative
stimulates
Concept construction
Thinking
Attitudes
Process skills
Experiences
Specific, well planned
Stimulate learners
Teachers
Students
can be
Deduction
Explicit teaching method
Improved
Four Steps
Ten steps
by
Enhancing, supplementing
Resequencing
Selection

TRANSPARENCY MASTERS by chapter

Chapter 1: ***Teaching Science For All Children***
Martin & Sexton © 1997 by Allyn and Bacon

Chapter 1: What Is Science?

Central concepts:

- considerable improvements in science achievement have been made during past 10 years, yet present conditions and majority of teaching practices suppress gains in achievement
- science is a dynamic human enterprise, not a static construct
- as defined, science consists of three interrelated parts - attitudes, processes and knowledge
- "whole science" is the interrelationship of all three parts
- National Science Education Standards advocate scientific literacy for all learners through a whole science philosophy and teaching approach

T 1.0

Children's Perceptions

Science is ...

- "Real hard. Harder than reading. We aren't allowed to have it in kindergarten." (Antonio - K)
- "After lunch sometimes when there is nothing else to do." (Shawna, 1st)
- "When you smoke cigarettes and get cancer it is because of science." (Nancy, 1st)
- "We just read a book. I think you get it in junior high...." (William, 3rd)
- "It depends on what grade you're in and who your teacher is." (Greg, 5th)
- "Supposed to be about learning how we learn about the world and how to use the scientific method in thinking. I know because my dad is a scientist and he keeps asking me when we're going to learn that in science. I just tell him that we haven't gotten to it yet." (Doreen, 6th)

T 1.1

Children's Perceptions, cont.

"Scientists are ...

... middle aged white males who wear lab coats and glasses. Their peculiar facial features are indicative of their generally deranged behavior. They work indoors, alone, perhaps underground, surrounded by smoking test tubes and other pieces of technology. An air of secrecy and danger surrounds their work." (p. 6)

T 1.2

Science Proficiency

- International comparisons show that:
- United States' elementary children rank 9th out of 12 countries
- United States' secondary students rank last in most popular science course: Biology

T 1.3

Present Indicators

Considerable progress has been made in science education:

- the average amount of classroom time per day for science in grades 1 - 6 rose substantially between 1977 and 1993
- students' early exposure to science benefits them through high school far more than in the past
- the number of women receiving bachelors degrees in science fields increased from 29% to 44% between 1971 and 1991, and the doctoral degrees in science for women increased from 10% to 28%, while the number of men receiving doctoral degrees remained the same

(Source: Suter, L. E (ed.) (1996). ~~The learning curve: What we are discovering about U.S. science and mathematics education.~~ (NSF 96-53). National Science Foundation: Washington, D.C., p. 2)

T 1.4

Student Achievement

Science proficiency scores have improved, overall, since 1977.

Students scored at or above the 250 item-type level on the National Assessment of Educational Progress (NAEP) test.

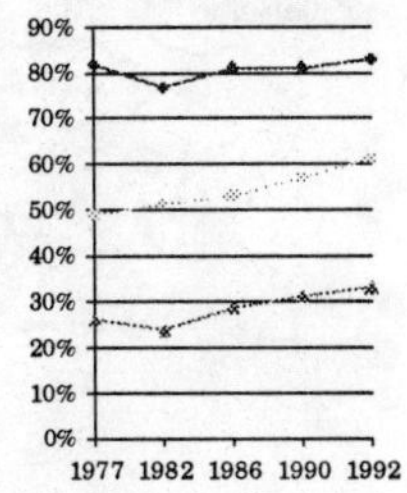

(Source: Suter, L. E (ed.) (1996). ~~The learning curve: What we are discovering about U.S. science and mathematics education.~~ (NSF 96-53). National Science Foundation: Washington, D.C., p. 8)

T 1.5

Chapter 1: ***Teaching Science For All Children***
Martin & Sexton © 1997 by Allyn and Bacon

U. S. Comparisons

- students have high scores on remembering content
- low scores on using content to analyze and problem-solve
- youth who are minorities and/or disadvantaged score lower than urban whites
- Black, Hispanics and Native Americans remain underrepresented in science and engineering careers representative to their presence in the overall college-age population.
- young children like science, though half of their schools have it as a priority
- older youth dislike science

Average Teaching Minutes

Average number of minutes per day spent teaching each subject to self-contained classes for grades 1 - 3.

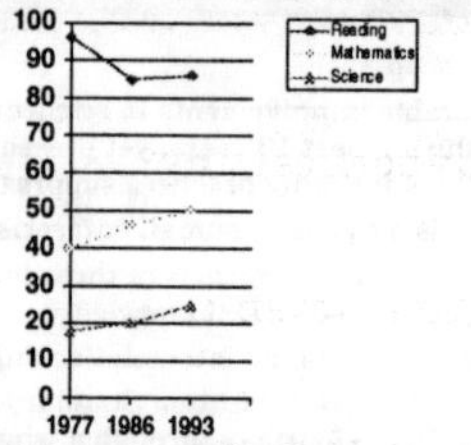

(Source: Suter, L. E (ed.) (1996). The learning curve: What we are discovering about U.S. science and mathematics education. (NSF 96-53). National Science Foundation: Washington, D.C., p. 11)

Average Teaching Minutes

Average number of minutes per day spent teaching each subject to self-contained classes for grades 4 - 6.

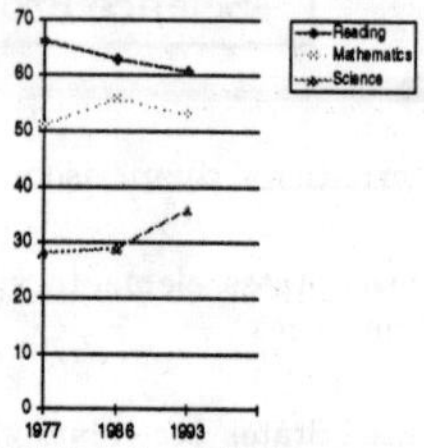

(Source: Suter, L. E (ed.) (1996). The learning curve: What we are discovering about U.S. science and mathematics education. (NSF 96-53). National Science Foundation: Washington, D.C., p. 11)

What is science?

Science is a concept constructed from human activity. Out of our curiosity, our need to know and the ways we seek, we make discoveries.

Science is the interrelationship of these three factors: attitudes, processes, and knowledge.

Scientific Attitudes

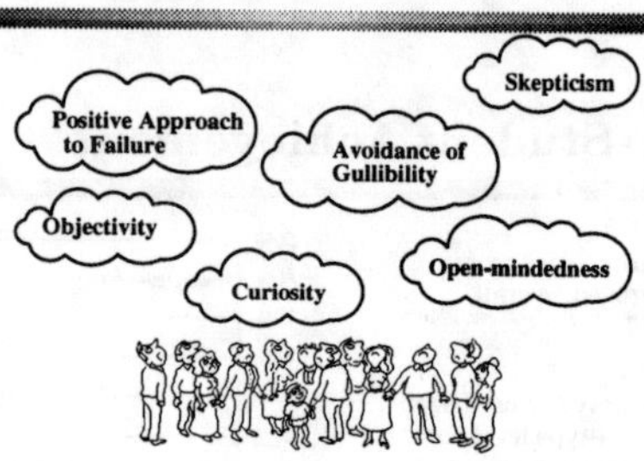

Scientific Processes include Basic Skills such as:

- Observing
- Classifying
- Measuring

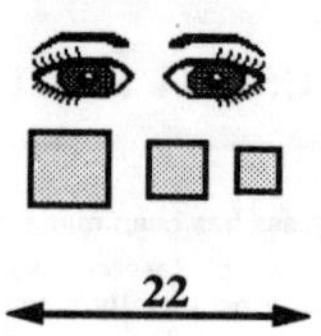

Scientific Processes
include Integrated Skills such as:

- Hypothesizing — **If ... Then ...**
- Experimenting

- Investigating

Science Knowledge includes:

- Facts
- Concepts
- Principles
- Theories

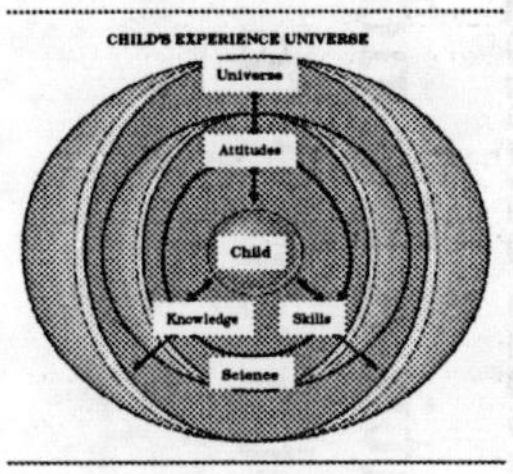

Fig. 1.3

Whole Science

Formula from the ***National Science Education Standards***:

Whole Science = Attitudes
+ Processes
+ Knowledge

Whole Science ⇨ Scientific Literacy

Chapter 1: What Is Science?

Central concepts:

- considerable improvements in science achievement have been made during past 10 years, yet present conditions and majority of teaching practices suppress gains in achievement
- science is a dynamic human enterprise, not a static construct
- as defined, science consists of three interrelated parts - attitudes, processes and knowledge
- "whole science" is the interrelationship of all three parts
- National Science Education Standards advocate scientific literacy for all learners through a whole science philosophy and teaching approach

Children's Perceptions

Science is ...

- "Real hard. Harder than reading. We aren't allowed to have it in kindergarten." (Antonio - K)
- "After lunch sometimes when there is nothing else to do." (Shawna, 1st)
- "When you smoke cigarettes and get cancer it is because of science." (Nancy, 1st)
- "We just read a book. I think you get it in junior high...." (William, 3rd)
- "It depends on what grade you're in and who your teacher is." (Greg, 5th)
- "Supposed to be about learning how we learn about the world and how to use the scientific method in thinking. I know because my dad is a scientist and he keeps asking me when we're going to learn that in science. I just tell him that we haven't gotten to it yet." (Doreen, 6th)

Children's Perceptions, cont.

"Scientists are ...

... middle aged white males who wear lab coats and glasses. Their peculiar facial features are indicative of their generally deranged behavior. They work indoors, alone, perhaps underground, surrounded by smoking test tubes and other pieces of technology. An air of secrecy and danger surrounds their work." (p. 6)

Science Proficiency

- <u>International comparisons</u> show that:
- United States' elementary children rank 9th out of 12 countries
- United States' secondary students rank last in most popular science course: Biology

Present Indicators

Considerable progress has been made in science education:

- the average amount of classroom time per day for science in grades 1 - 6 rose substantially between 1977 and 1993
- students' early exposure to science benefits them through high school far more than in the past
- the number of women receiving bachelors degrees in science fields increased from 29% to 44% between 1971 and 1991, and the doctoral degrees in science for women increased from 10% to 28%, while the number of men receiving doctoral degrees remained the same

(Source: Suter, L. E (ed.) (1996). The learning curve: What we are discovering about U.S. science and mathematics education. (NSF 96-53). National Science Foundation: Washington, D.C., p. 2)

Student Achievement

Science proficiency scores have improved, overall, since 1977.

Students scored at or above the 250 item-type level on the National Assessment of Educational Progress (NAEP) test.

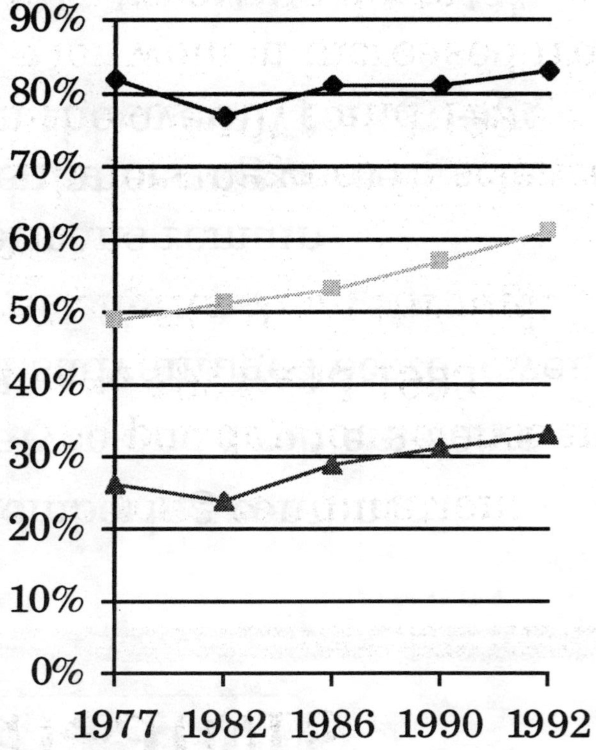

(Source: Suter, L. E (ed.) (1996). The learning curve: What we are discovering about U.S. science and mathematics education. (NSF 96-53). National Science Foundation: Washington, D.C., p. 8)

U. S. Comparisons

- students have high scores on remembering content
- low scores on <u>using</u> content to analyze and problem-solve
- youth who are minorities and/or disadvantaged score lower than urban whites
- Black, Hispanics and Native Americans remain underrepresented in science and engineering careers representative to their presence in the overall college-age population.
- young children like science, though half of their schools have it as a priority
- older youth dislike science

Average Teaching Minutes

Average number of minutes per day spent teaching each subject to self-contained classes for grades 1 - 3.

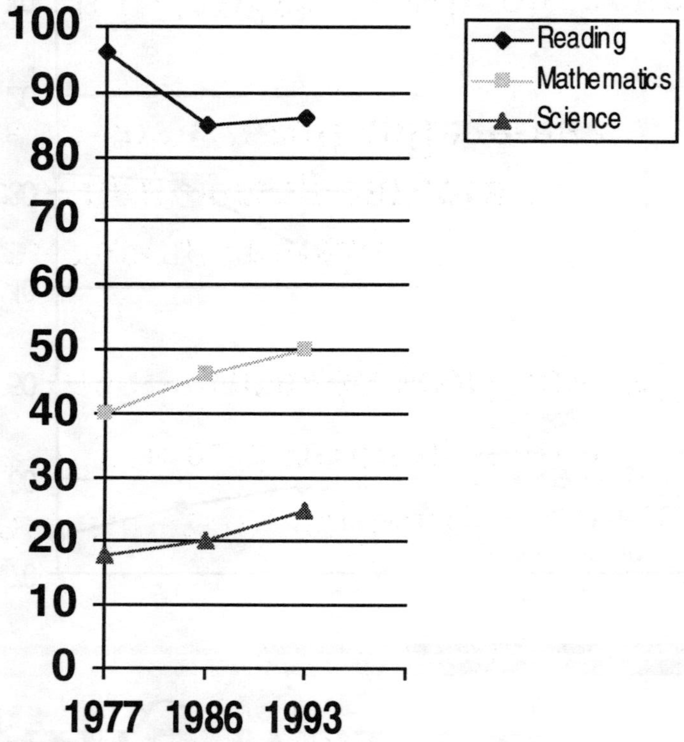

(Source: Suter, L. E (ed.) (1996). The learning curve: What we are discovering about U.S. science and mathematics education. (NSF 96-53). National Science Foundation: Washington, D.C., p. 11)

Average Teaching Minutes

Average number of minutes per day spent teaching each subject to self-contained classes for grades 4 - 6.

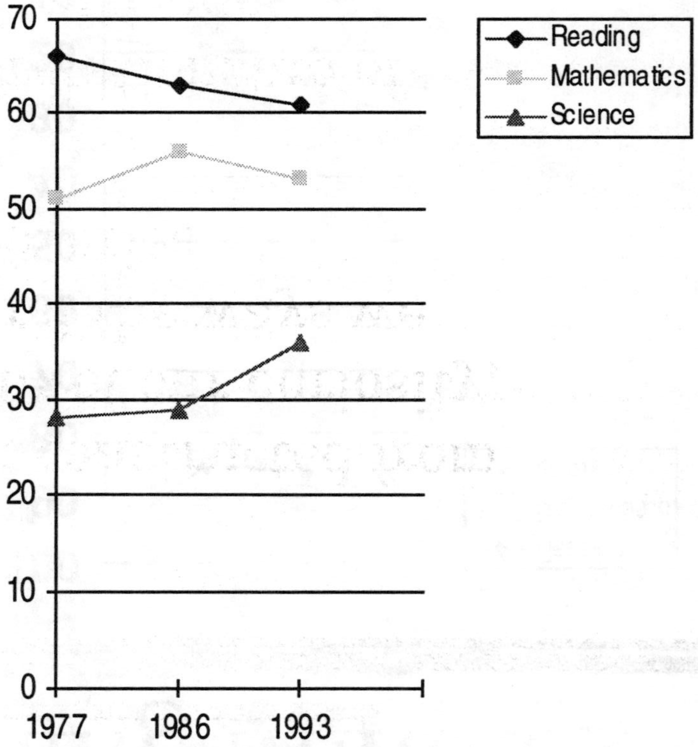

(Source: Suter, L. E (ed.) (1996). The learning curve: What we are discovering about U.S. science and mathematics education. (NSF 96-53). National Science Foundation: Washington, D.C., p. 11)

What is science?

Science is a concept constructed from human activity. Out of our curiosity, our need to know and the ways we seek, we make discoveries.

Science is the interrelationship of these three factors: attitudes, processes, and knowledge.

Scientific Attitudes

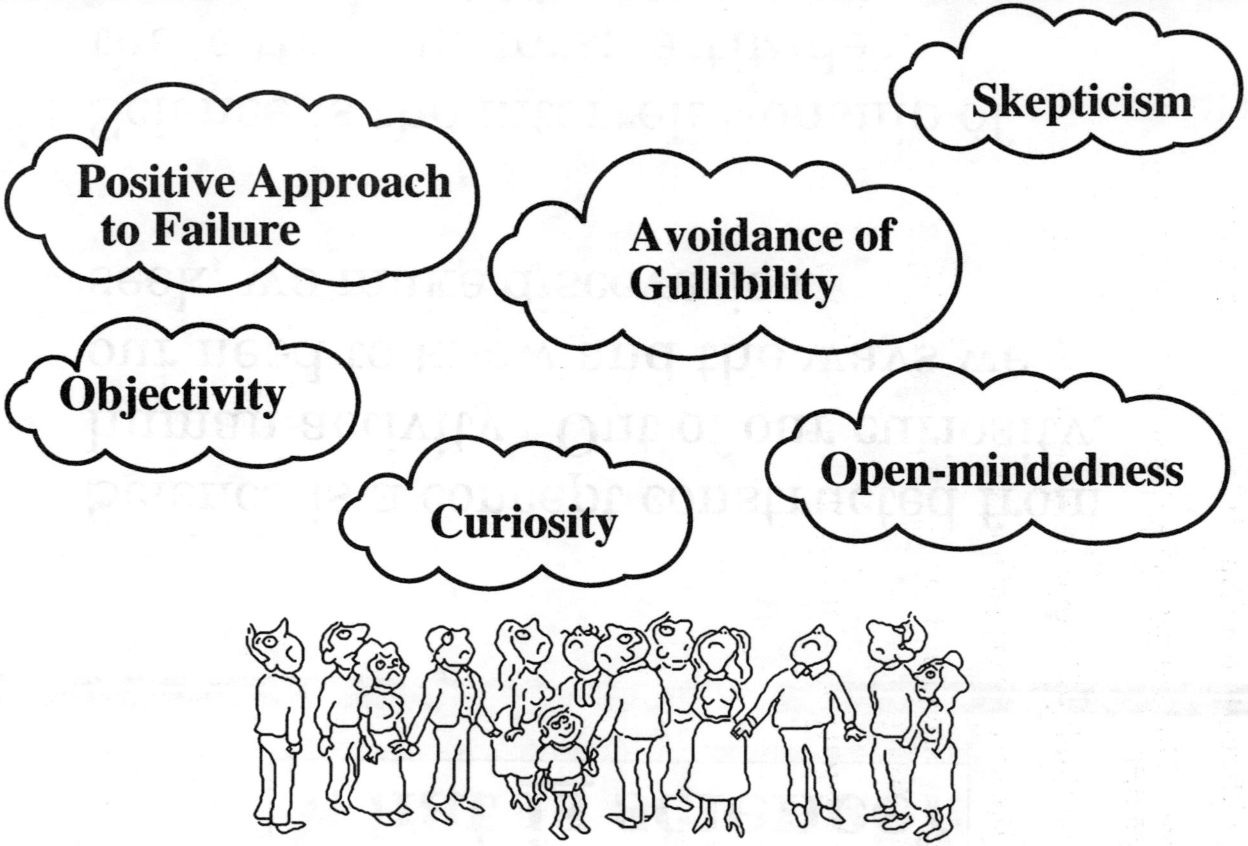

Scientific Processes
include <u>Basic Skills</u> such as:

- Observing

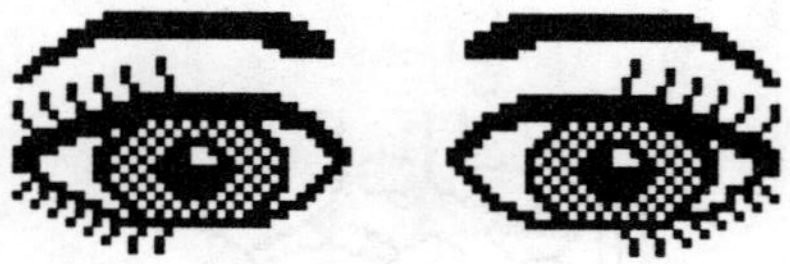

- Classifying

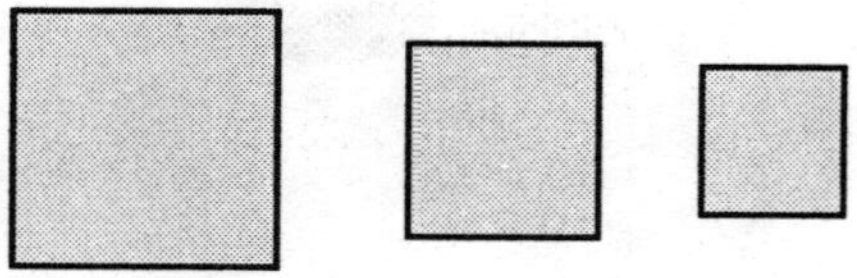

- Measuring

Scientific Processes
include <u>Integrated Skills</u> such as:

- Hypothesizing
- Experimenting
- Investigating

If ... Then ...

Science Knowledge includes:

- Facts
- Concepts
- Principles
- Theories

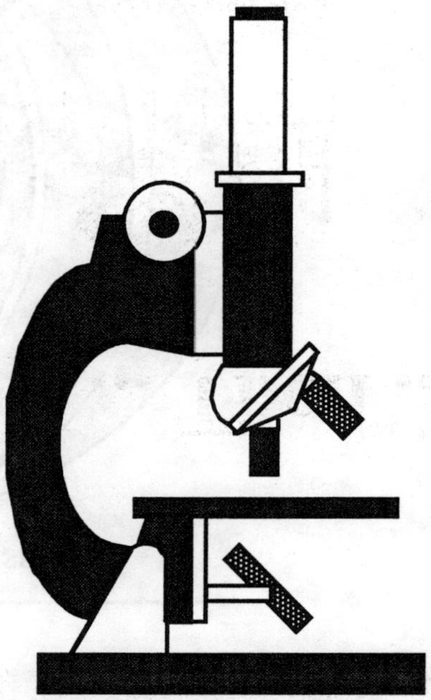

CHILD'S EXPERIENCE UNIVERSE

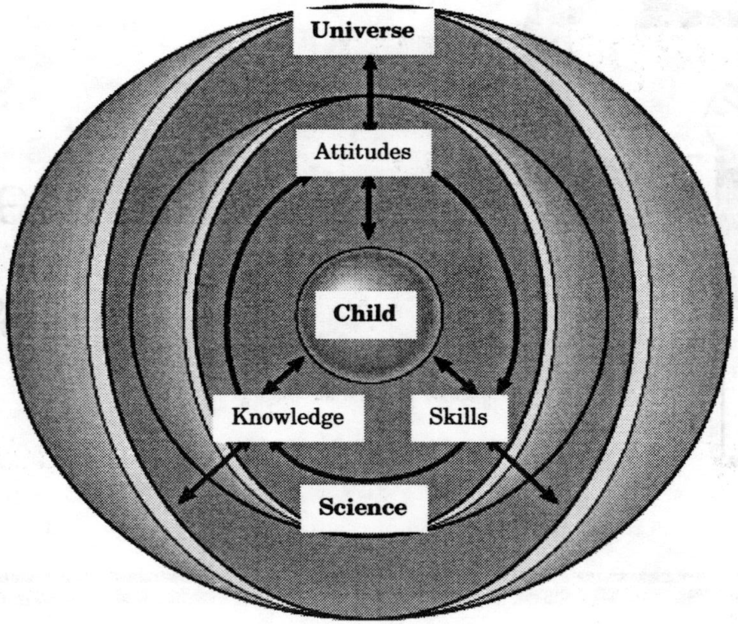

Fig. 1.3

Whole Science

Formula from the ***National Science Education Standards***:

Whole Science = Attitudes

\+ Processes

\+ Knowledge

Whole Science ⇨ Scientific Literacy

Chapter 2: ***Teaching Science For All Children***
Martin & Sexton © 1997 by Allyn and Bacon

Chapter 2: How Do Children Learn Science?

Central concepts:

- children's prior ideas and pre/mis/conceptions influence new learning
- children's needs affect what and how they learn
- a global synthesis of theories is used to explain how we now believe children learn
- children's experiences help them construct what they learn; constructivist views range in intensity
- constructivism is supported by many techniques and teacher roles

What Ideas Influence Childrens' Learning?

- Preconceptions
- Misconceptions
- Conceptions

Preconceptions are ...

- ideas that children bring with them from prior experiences
- often incomplete preliminary understandings of fundamental science concepts
- children's attempts to explain their natural world
- influenced by hands-on, minds-on experiences, including the physical, emotional, social
- thoughtful efforts to make (construct) sense
- influenced by bias and culture

Misconceptions

- are common and represent explanations of phenomena constructed by a student as a response to a prior experience
- are alternative understandings that are scientifically incorrect and may be based on simple inaccurate comprehension of an event, reason, or explanation (see Table 2.1)
- may take a long time to correct, but can be avoided when concepts are constructed carefully from experiences
- can be revealed through specific science experiences that are accompanied by dialogue

Children's Ideas

- are personal, diverse, and constructed from direct experiences
- may seem contradictory, inconsistent, and incoherent to an adult
- are persistent, resistant to change and durable

Children's Needs

- stimulate thinking (use 5 senses)
- encourage physical activity
- develop language skills
- stimulate socialization
- build self-esteem
- fit their own pace (time factor)

Chapter 2: ***Teaching Science For All Children***
Martin & Sexton © 1997 by Allyn and Bacon

The Dominant Perspective

Constructivism is the general name of the dominant perspective on learning in science education. Constructivism emphasizes the active role of the learner: mentally, physically, and socially.

Constructivism

a contemporary perspective on science learning

"A theory that assumes knowledge cannot exist outside the learner ... [and that] knowledge is a construction of the learner's reality."

Figure 2.1 Constructivism Continuum

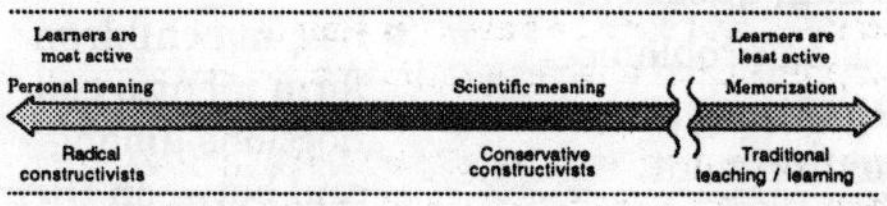

Constructivist Teachers

Strive to accomplish three things:

- use or create learning opportunities that are meaningful to children
- encourage children to make real decisions
- encourage peers to exchange views in order to refine thinking and deepen understanding

Jean Piaget

Swiss biologist and psychologist

- **theory of cognitive development, not of learning**
- **believed information accumulated in the mind to form structures**
- **progressive (and concurrent) stage development**
- **stages are:**
  - sensorimotor
  - pre-operational
  - concrete
  - formal

Jean Piaget, continued

- **thesis of the theory revolves around "Equilibration" where experience (external and internal) can create dilemmas and mental conflict; learner is biologically driven to regain equilibrium (Figs. 2.2, 2.3)**
- **"Assimilation" is adapting new information to structures formed from prior experiences**
- **"Accommodation" is the formation of new (and perhaps temporary) mental structures)**

Chapter 2: ***Teaching Science For All Children***
Martin & Sexton © 1997 by Allyn and Bacon

Figure 2.2 Equilibrium Model

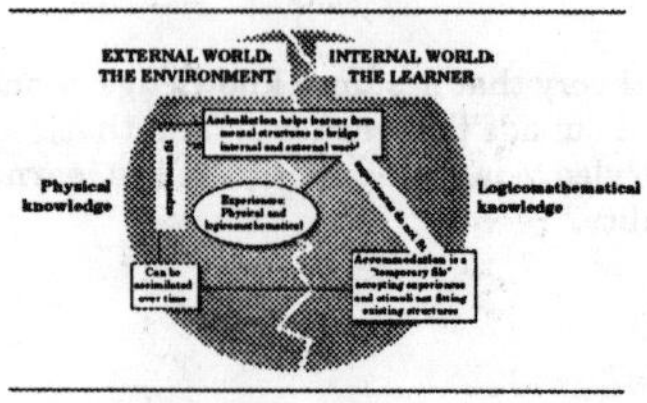

Fig. 2.3 **Science Education Learning Model**

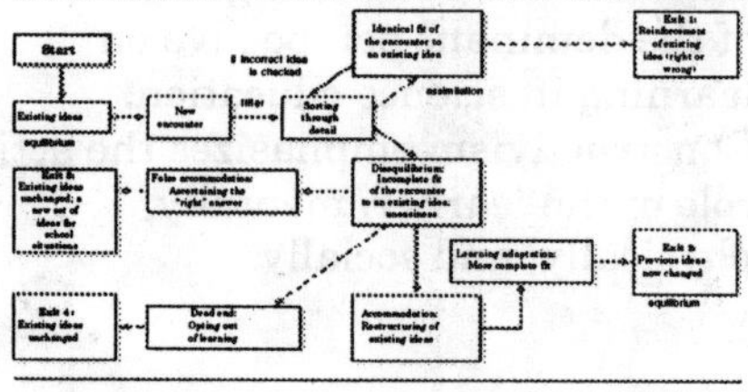

Constructivist Teachers

- **advocate hands-on, minds-on learning to promote the interplay of what is already known and what new ideas will be formed**
- **value prior ideas of children**
- **urge students to identify mental discrepancies linked to prior ideas, correct for proper concept formation**

Constructivist Teaching Methods

- **presenting**
- **observing**
- **asking questions**
- **posing problems**
- **organizing class environment**
- **coordinating class human relations**
- **assessing and documenting learning**
- **helping children form mental connections among and between their ideas**

(see Figure 2.5, 2.6)

Constructivist Learning and Teaching Model

Figure 2.4

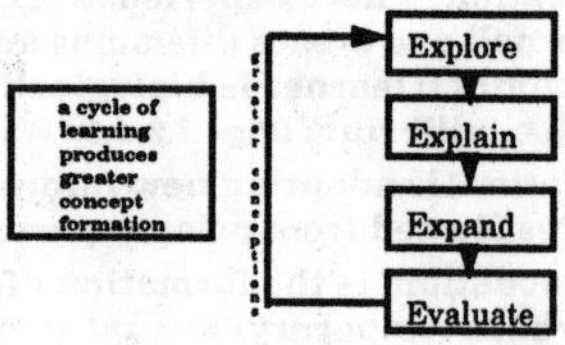

Chapter 2: How Do Children Learn Science?

Central concepts:

- children's prior ideas and pre/mis/conceptions influence new learning
- children's needs affect what and how they learn
- a global synthesis of theories is used to explain how we now believe children learn
- children's experiences help them construct what they learn; constructivist views range in intensity
- constructivism is supported by many techniques and teacher roles

What Ideas Influence Childrens' Learning?

- Preconceptions
- Misconceptions
- Conceptions

Preconceptions are ...

- ideas that children bring with them from prior experiences
- often incomplete preliminary understandings of fundamental science concepts
- children's attempts to explain their natural world
- influenced by hands-on, minds-on experiences, including the physical, emotional, social
- thoughtful efforts to make (construct) sense
- influenced by bias and culture

Misconceptions

- are common and represent explanations of phenomena constructed by a student as a response to a prior experience
- are alternative understandings that are scientifically incorrect and may be based on simple inaccurate comprehension of an event, reason, or explanation (see Table 2.1)
- may take a long time to correct, but can be avoided when concepts are constructed carefully from experiences
- can be revealed through specific science experiences that are accompanied by dialogue

Children's Ideas

- are <u>personal</u>, diverse, and constructed from direct experiences
- may seem <u>contradictory</u>, inconsistent, and incoherent to an adult
- are <u>persistent</u>, resistant to change and durable

Children's Needs

- stimulate <u>thinking</u> (use 5 senses)
- encourage <u>physical activity</u>
- develop <u>language</u> skills
- stimulate <u>socialization</u>
- build <u>self-esteem</u>
- fit their own pace (<u>time</u> factor)

The Dominant Perspective

Constructivism is the general name of the dominant perspective on learning in science education. Constructivism emphasizes the <u>active</u> role of the learner: mentally, physically, and socially.

Constructivism

a contemporary perspective on science learning

"A theory that assumes knowledge cannot exist outside the learner ... [and that] knowledge is a construction of the learner's reality."

Figure 2.1 Constructivism Continuum

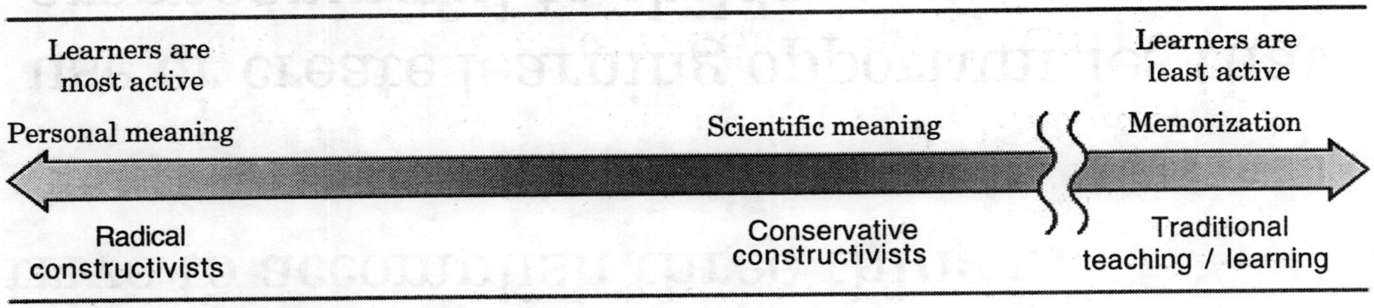

Constructivist Teachers

Strive to accomplish three things:

- use or create learning opportunities that are meaningful to children
- encourage children to make real decisions
- encourage peers to exchange views in order to refine thinking and deepen understanding

Jean Piaget

Swiss biologist and psychologist

- **theory of cognitive development, not of learning**
- **believed information accumulated in the mind to form structures**
- **progressive (and concurrent) stage development**
- **stages are:**
  - sensorimotor
  - pre-operational
  - concrete
  - formal

Jean Piaget, continued

- thesis of the theory revolves around "Equilibration" where experience (external and internal) can create dilemmas and mental conflict; learner is biologically driven to regain equilibrium (Figs. 2.2, 2.3)
- "Assimilation" is adapting new information to structures formed from prior experiences
- "Accommodation" is the formation of new (and perhaps temporary) mental structures)

Figure 2.2 Equilibrium Model

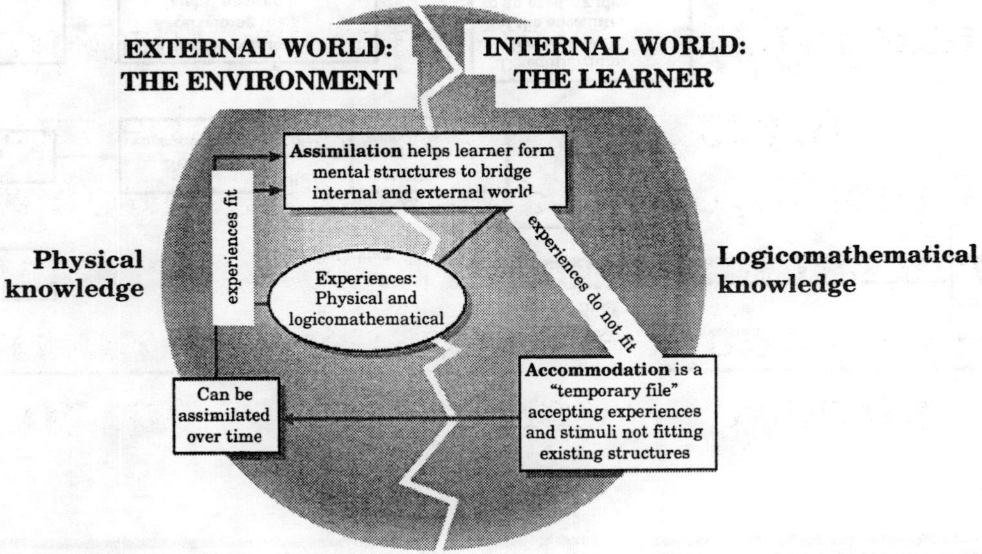

Fig. 2.3 **Science Education Learning Model**

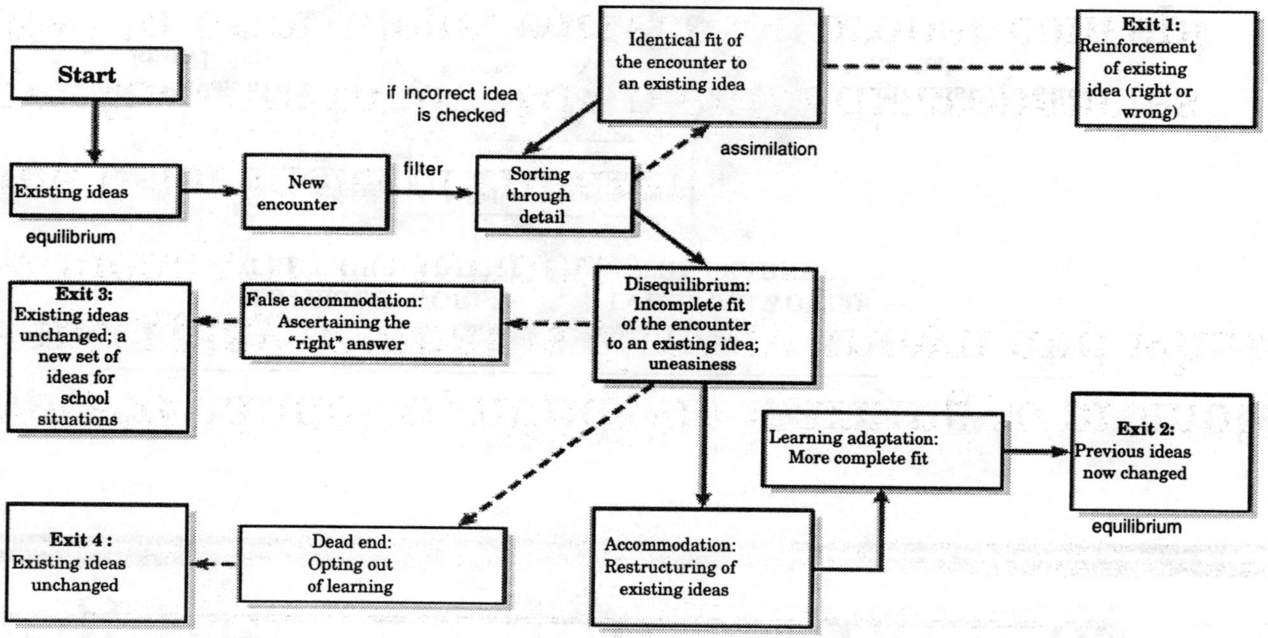

Constructivist Teachers

- advocate hands-on, minds-on learning to promote the interplay of what is already known and what new ideas will be formed
- value prior ideas of children
- urge students to identify mental discrepancies linked to prior ideas, correct for proper concept formation

Constructivist Teaching Methods

- presenting
- observing
- asking questions
- posing problems
- organizing class environment
- coordinating class human relations
- assessing and documenting learning
- helping children form mental connections among and between their ideas

(see Figure 2.5, 2.6)

Constructivist Learning and Teaching Model

Figure 2.4

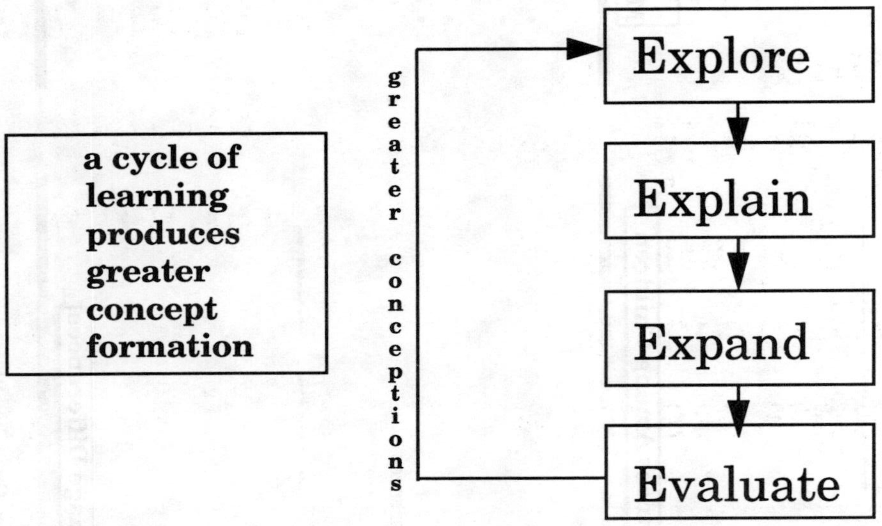

Chapter 3: *Teaching Science For All Children*

Martin & Sexton © 1997 by Allyn and Bacon

Chapter 3: How Can You Teach *All* Children?

Central concepts:

- science is for all irrespective of differences in culture, language, gender, learning style, or exceptionality
- all children can learn and benefit from science if taught in a way that is consistent with their capabilities
- parents can help teachers meet children's special needs

T 3.0

 Teaching Science For All Children

Science For All Children

Science is essential for:

- developing basic skills
- bridging cultural differences
- constructing or strengthening language
- overcoming gender stereotypes
- accommodating learning (style) preferences

T 3.1

 Teaching Science For All Children

Multiple Cultures Among Children

Include:

- race
- religion
- ethnicity
- economics
- language differences
- gender

T 3.2

 Teaching Science For All Children

NSTA Position Statement on Multicultural Science Education

- provide access and experiences for all children
- select/use materials and strategies that encourage diversity
- become aware of learning style preferences
- expose all children to career/technology opportunities

T 3.3

 Teaching Science For All Children

Language Differences

- try "Demonstrate - Group Investigate - Individual Investigate" teaching model (Table 3.1)
- focus instruction and assignments on "language functions" (Table 3.2)
- encourage use of study aids to help students help themselves
- stimulate physical learning
- reduce test anxiety

T 3.4

 Teaching Science For All Children

Gender

- unequal access, sex-role stereotypes
- cultural disincentives, insufficient background
- teachers influence sex-role stereotypes
- Cooper's model for overcoming stereotypes (Fig. 3.1)
- steps for overcoming inequality
  - grouping - expectations - role models
  - stronger preparation - aware of bias

T 3.5

 Teaching Science For All Children

Chapter 3: ***Teaching Science For All Children***
Martin & Sexton © 1997 by Allyn and Bacon

Figure 3.1 Gender Equity

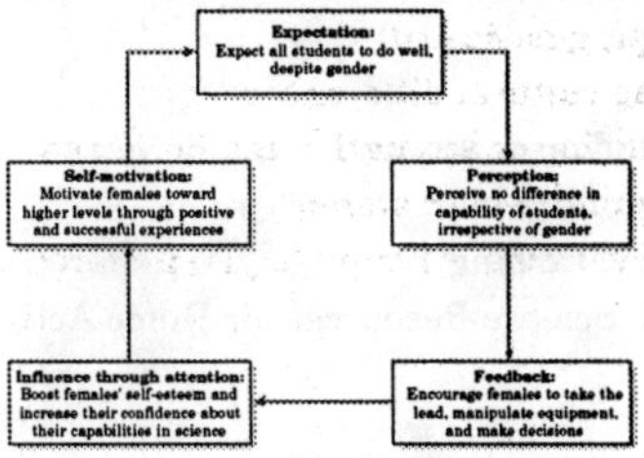

Table 3.3 **Bringing Gender Balance to Your Science Lessons**

- connect science and technology to the real world
- choose metaphors carefully; have students develop their own
- foster collaboration
- encourage females to act as experts
- have females control the classroom technology
- portray technology as a way to solve problems
- capitalize on females' verbal strengths
- experiment with testing and evaluation
- give frequent feedback, keep expectations high
- experiment with note-taking techniques

Learning Styles

Learners may be classified as:

- visuals - "show me!"
- listeners - " tell me!"
- kinesthetics - "let me do it!"
- loners - "let me do it by myself!"
- groupies - "let us do it!"
- verbals - "let me tell you!"
- writers - "I'll write it for you!"
- sequentials - "step-by-step!"
- globals - "I have the big idea!"

Teaching Tips for Helping *All* Learners

- approach each topic in many different ways
- provide abundant opportunities for hands-on
- support vocabulary and reading development

Teaching Tips for Helping *All* Learners, continued

- be organized and actively supervise
- use cross-cultural buddy systems and cooperative groups
- use visual and listening aids
- maintain high expectations for all

Exceptional Learners

Include children who have:

- Learning Disabilities
- Intellectual Handicaps
- Physical Disabilities
- Talents and/or Intellectual Gifts

Table 3.4 provides suggestions for adapting: the class environment, materials, teaching methods, assessment

Figure 3.2 Conceptual Development

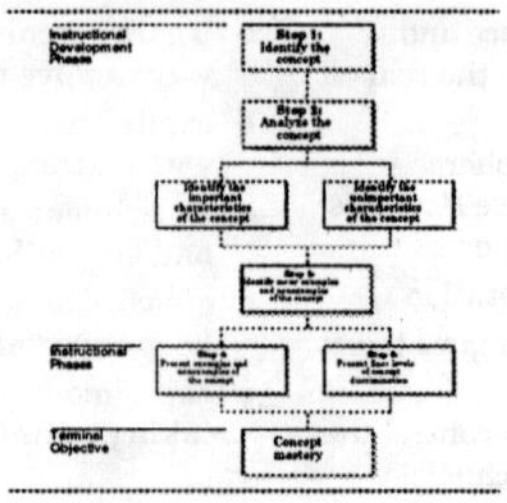

Encourage Parents to Help Children Learn Science

Science is important because:

- employment
- income
- career advancement
- quality of life
- life-long learning

Table 3.5 Science Resources for Home Activities

Chapter 3: How Can You Teach *All* Children?

Central concepts:

- science is for all irrespective of differences in culture, language, gender, learning style, or exceptionality
- all children can learn and benefit from science if taught in a way that is consistent with their capabilities
- parents can help teachers meet children's special needs

Science For <u>All</u> Children

Science is essential for:

- developing basic skills
- bridging cultural differences
- constructing or strengthening language
- overcoming gender stereotypes
- accommodating learning (style) preferences

Multiple Cultures Among Children

Include:

- race
- religion
- ethnicity
- economics
- language differences
- gender

NSTA Position Statement on Multicultural Science Education

- provide access and experiences for <u>all</u> children
- select/use materials and strategies that encourage diversity
- become aware of learning style preferences
- expose <u>all</u> children to career/technology opportunities

Language Differences

- try "Demonstrate - Group Investigate - Individual Investigate" teaching model (Table 3.1)
- focus instruction and assignments on "language functions" (Table 3.2)
- encourage use of study aids to help students help themselves
- stimulate physical learning
- reduce test anxiety

Gender

- unequal access, sex-role stereotypes
- cultural disincentives, insufficient background
- teachers influence sex-role stereotypes
- Cooper's model for overcoming stereotypes (Fig. 3.1)
- steps for overcoming inequality
  - grouping
  - expectations
  - role models
  - stronger preparation
  - aware of bias

Figure 3.1 Gender Equity

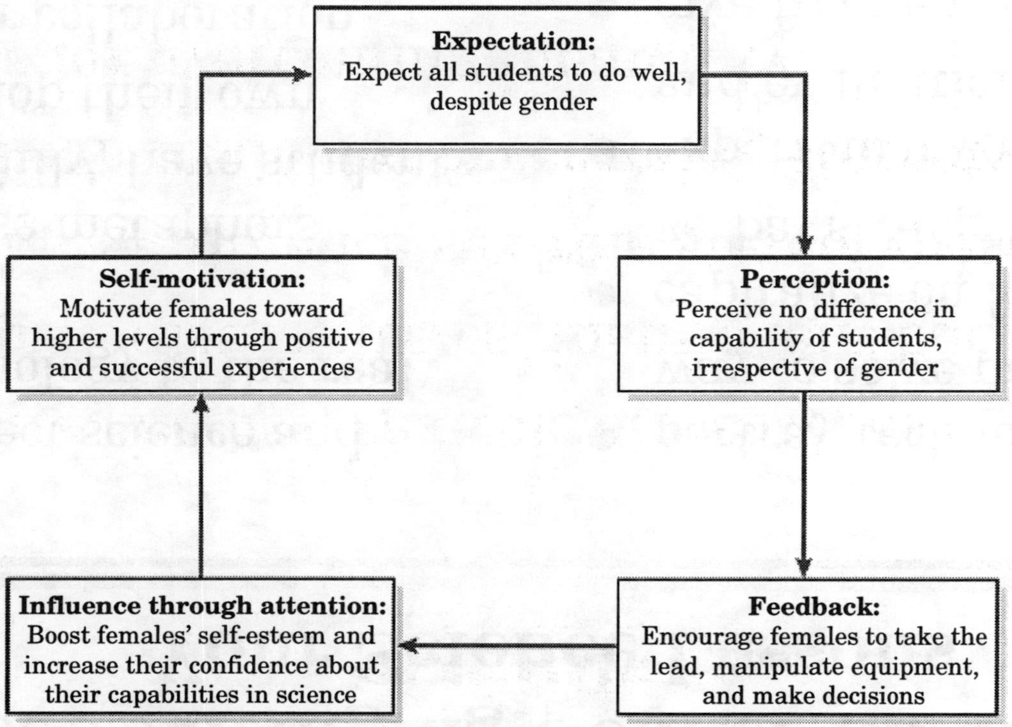

Table 3.3 **Bringing Gender Balance to Your Science Lessons**

- connect science and technology to the real world
- choose metaphors carefully; have students develop their own
- foster collaboration
- encourage females to act as experts
- have females control the classroom technology
- portray technology as a way to solve problems
- capitalize on females' verbal strengths
- experiment with testing and evaluation
- give frequent feedback, keep expectations high
- experiment with note-taking techniques

Learning Styles

Learners may be classified as:

- visuals - "show me!"
- listeners - " tell me!"
- kinesthetics - "let me do it!"
- loners - "let me do it by myself!"
- groupies - "let us do it!"
- verbals - "let me tell you!"
- writers - "I'll write it for you!"
- sequentials - "step-by-step!"
- globals - "I have the big idea!"

Teaching Tips for Helping *All* Learners

- approach each topic in many different ways
- provide abundant opportunities for hands-on
- support vocabulary and reading development

Teaching Tips for Helping *All* Learners, continued

- be organized and actively supervise
- use cross-cultural buddy systems and cooperative groups
- use visual and listening aids
- maintain high expectations for all

Exceptional Learners

Include children who have:

- Learning Disabilities
- Intellectual Handicaps
- Physical Disabilities
- Talents and/or Intellectual Gifts

Table 3.4 provides suggestions for adapting: the class environment, materials, teaching methods, assessment

Figure 3.2 Conceptual Development

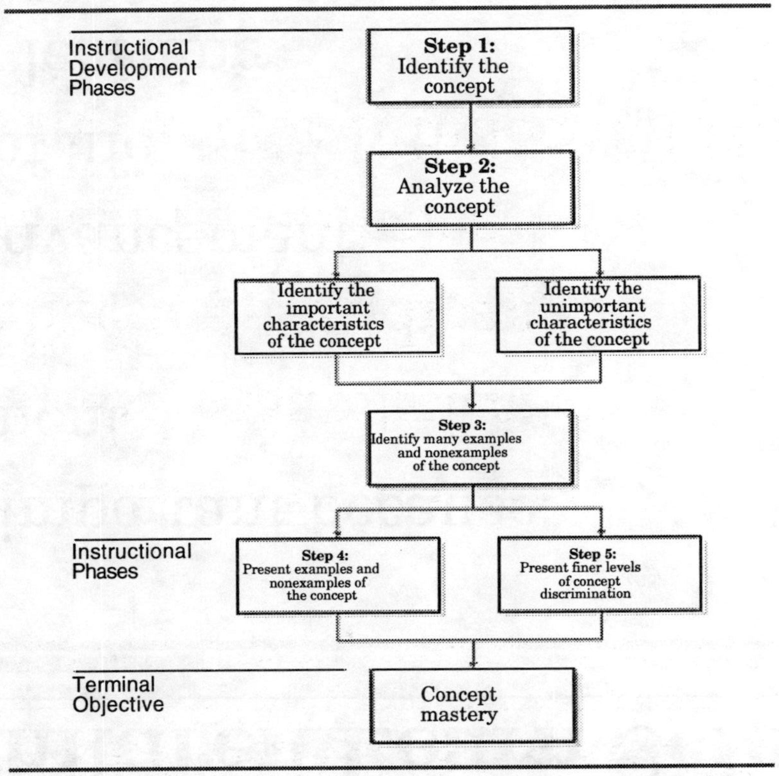

Encourage Parents to Help Children Learn Science

Science is important because:

- employment
- income
- career advancement
- quality of life
- life-long learning

Table 3.5 Science Resources for Home Activities

Chapter 4: ***Teaching Science For All Children***
Martin & Sexton © 1997 by Allyn and Bacon

Chapter 4: What Goals Promote Scientific Literacy?

Central concepts:

- science is a basic subject and affects our lives
- reform efforts attempt to meet children's needs in a changing society
- new science program and teaching goals arise from extensive research and collaboration
- new science goals support whole science concept
- National Science Education Standards provide new dimensions and outcomes

What Is Scientific Literacy?

According to the National Research Council, **literacy means**:

- a person can ask for and determine answers to questions stimulated by curiosity
- the ability to describe, explain, and predict natural phenomena
- the ability to read and understand scientific articles in the popular press and converse about validity of conclusions
- a person can identify scientific issues and express positions that underlie national and local decisions
- a person can evaluate the quality of scientific information of its sources and methods
- a capacity to pose and evaluate arguments based on evidence and conclusions

Science Attitudes

- promote creativity
- encourage creative writing
- are the foundation for good health habits
- develop mathematical skills
- provide experiences that can be the inspiration for art and music
- develop reading and social studies skills
- feed development of self-esteem (see Figure 4.1)

Science Process Skills

The crucial tools of today's human living include those skills that allow us to adapt ourselves to our environment -- to live with uncertainty and tolerate ambiguity -- and to adapt our environment to ourselves -- to analyze, synthesize, and hypothesize. These "process-oriented" skills are literacy building tools that are vital to adult living.

Science Process Skills

- provide the type and quality of science experiences for children
- are as important for constructing an understanding of science content
- support learning in other school subjects
- have value in and out of school and are skills that foster life-long learning

Project Synthesis

National research findings revealed:

- lack of support for science instruction
- textbooks dominated what science is taught
- school goals largely emphasized science content in preparation for next grade level
- teachers were the curriculum and often did not use effective science teaching practices or work toward national agendas

Project Synthesis, continued

Four Outcomes:
- Use science to enhance each learner's Personal Development
- Help learners to understand the Interrelationships of Science, Technology and Society
- Use science to develop each learner's Academic and Process Skills
- Use science to help expand each learner's Career Awareness

T 4.6

Scope, Sequence & Coordination

- SS&C is a project of the NSTA for Middle and Secondary schools
- strives to eliminate the "layer cake" separation of the sciences into individual disconnected courses, e.g., biology, chemistry, physics, earth/space science
- proposed that each student study each science field each year for six years
- use constructivist teaching and learning approaches to focus on the major concepts
- uses themes as instructional organizers
- pilot tests show that student are developing affinity for science, rather than fear

T 4.7

Project 2061

Selected principles:
- select science content carefully and for a common core
- encourage diversity and serve needs of all students
- emphasize science concepts
- accomplish learning outcomes through constructivist practices
- form a selective and integrated curriculum organized around themes
- address social and technological issues
- base instruction on explicit criteria

T 4.8

National Science Education Standards

- the first nation-wide, system-wide effort to reform science education
- goals are to prepare students who can:
  - use science attitudes, processes, and knowledge when making personal decisions
  - appreciate the attitudes and excitement of knowing about the natural world
  - use science to increase economic productivity
  - engage intelligently in public discourse and debate about science and technology matters

T 4.9

Goals of NSES

School science programs must provide experiences that:
- are personally and socially relevant to the child
- include a wide range of experiences so that students can analyze personal and societal issues critically
- encourage students to demonstrate understanding and impact that science has on their lives, society, and world
- encourage students to appreciate science
- help students to develop an appreciate for the beauty and order of the natural world

T 4.10

Figure 4.2 *NSES for Systemic Reform*

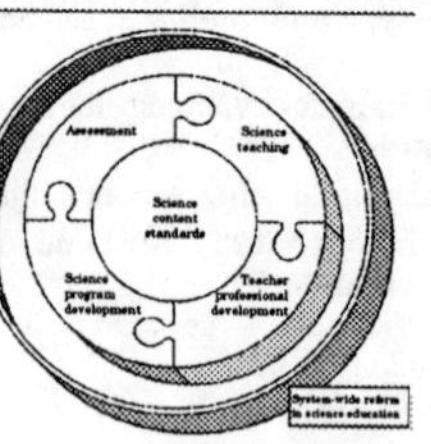

T 4.11

NSES Science Content Outcomes

4 New Dimensions of Science Content Goals:

- Science as Inquiry
- Science and Technology
- Science in Personal and Social Perspectives
- History and Nature of Science

Figure 4.3 NSES Content Dimensions

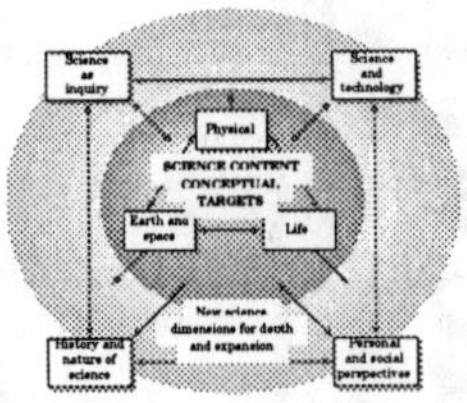

Dimension 1. *Science As Inquiry*

Learning outcomes from Table 4.3

1.1 Develop abilities necessary to do scientific inquiry.
- » ask questions, plan and conduct simple investigations use simple science equipment, etc.

1.2 Understand about scientific inquiry.
- » select the kind of investigation that fits the question, realize that instruments enhance senses, develop explanations from data, describe investigations that are repeatable, etc.

Dimension 2. *Science and Technology*

Learning outcomes from Table 4.3

2.1 Develop an ability to distinguish between natural and other objects made by humans.

2.2 Develop an ability to understand and produce a technological design.

2.3 Understand about the relationship between science and technology.

Dimension 3. *Science in Personal and Social Perspectives*

Learning outcomes from Table 4.3

3.1 Develop an understanding of personal health.
3.2 Identify characteristics and describe changes in populations.
3.3 Identify types of resources.
3.4 Identify environments and changes.
3.5 Recognize the benefits and challenges of science and technology.

Dimension 4. *History and Nature of Science*

Learning outcomes from Table 4.3

4.1 Understand that science is a human endeavor.

4.2 Understand the nature of science.

4.3 Understand the importance of history to science.

Chapter 4: What Goals Promote Scientific Literacy?

Central concepts:

- science is a basic subject and affects our lives
- reform efforts attempt to meet children's needs in a changing society
- new science program and teaching goals arise from extensive research and collaboration
- new science goals support whole science concept
- National Science Education Standards provide new dimensions and outcomes

What Is Scientific Literacy?

According to the National Research Council, **literacy means**:

- a person can ask for and determine answers to questions stimulated by curiosity
- the ability to describe, explain, and predict natural phenomena
- the ability to read and understand scientific articles in the popular press and converse about validity of conclusions
- a person can identify scientific issues and express positions that underlie national and local decisions
- a person can evaluate the quality of scientific information of its sources and methods
- a capacity to pose and evaluate arguments based on evidence and conclusions

Science Attitudes

- promote creativity
- encourage creative writing
- are the foundation for good health habits
- develop mathematical skills
- provide experiences that can be the inspiration for art and music
- develop reading and social studies skills
- feed development of self-esteem (see Figure 4.1)

Science Process Skills

The crucial tools of today's human living include those skills that allow us to adapt ourselves to our environment -- to live with uncertainty and tolerate ambiguity -- and to adapt our environment to ourselves -- to analyze, synthesize, and hypothesize. These "process-oriented" skills are literacy building tools that are vital to adult living.

Science Process Skills

- provide the type and quality of science experiences for children
- are as important for constructing an understanding of science content
- support learning in other school subjects
- have value in and out of school and are skills that foster life-long learning

Project Synthesis

National research findings revealed:

- lack of support for science instruction
- textbooks dominated what science is taught
- school goals largely emphasized science content in preparation for next grade level
- teachers <u>were</u> the curriculum and often did not use effective science teaching practices or work toward national agendas

Project Synthesis, continued

Four Outcomes:

- Use science to enhance each learner's Personal Development
- Help learners to understand the Interrelationships of Science, Technology and Society
- Use science to develop each learner's Academic and Process Skills
- Use science to help expand each learner's Career Awareness

Scope, Sequence & Coordination

- SS&C is a project of the NSTA for Middle and Secondary schools
- strives to eliminate the "layer cake" separation of the sciences into individual disconnected courses, e.g., biology, chemistry, physics, earth/space science
- proposed that each student study each science field each year for six years
- use constructivist teaching and learning approaches to focus on the major concepts
- uses themes as instructional organizers
- pilot tests show that student are developing affinity for science, rather than fear

Project 2061

Selected principles:

- select science content carefully and for a common core
- encourage diversity and serve needs of all students
- emphasize science concepts
- accomplish learning outcomes through constructivist practices
- form a selective and integrated curriculum organized around themes
- address social and technological issues
- base instruction on explicit criteria

National Science Education Standards

- the first nation-wide, system-wide effort to reform science education
- goals are to prepare students who can:
  - » use science attitudes, processes, and knowledge when making personal decisions
  - » appreciate the attitudes and excitement of knowing about the natural world
  - » use science to increase economic productivity
  - » engage intelligently in public discourse and debate about science and technology matters

Goals of NSES

School science programs must provide experiences that:

- are personally and socially relevant to the child
- include a wide range of experiences so that students can analyze personal and societal issues critically
- encourage students to demonstrate understanding and impact that science has on their lives, society, and world
- encourage students to appreciate science
- help students to develop an appreciate for the beauty and order of the natural world

Figure 4.2 *NSES for Systemic Reform*

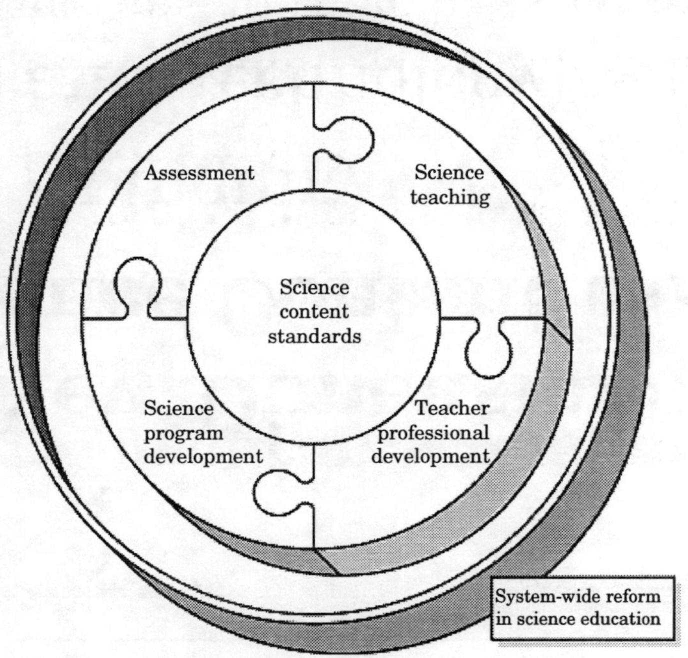

NSES *Science Content Outcomes*

4 New Dimensions of Science Content Goals:

- Science as Inquiry
- Science and Technology
- Science in Personal and Social Perspectives
- History and Nature of Science

Figure 4.3 NSES Content Dimensions

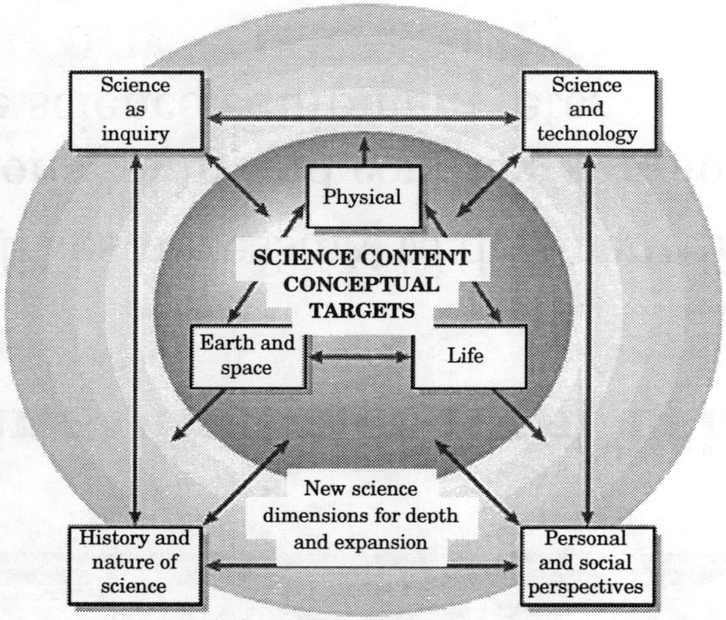

Dimension 1. *Science As Inquiry*

Learning outcomes from Table 4.3

1.1 Develop abilities necessary to do scientific inquiry.

» ask questions, plan and conduct simple investigations use simple science equipment, etc.

1.2 Understand about scientific inquiry.

» select the kind of investigation that fits the question, realize that instruments enhance senses, develop explanations from data, describe investigations that are repeatable, etc.

Dimension 2. *Science and Technology*

Learning outcomes from Table 4.3

2.1 Develop an ability to distinguish between natural and other objects made by humans.

2.2 Develop an ability to understand and produce a technological design.

2.3 Understand about the relationship between science and technology.

Dimension 3. *Science in Personal and Social Perspectives*

Learning outcomes from Table 4.3

3.1 Develop an understanding of personal health.

3.2 Identify characteristics and describe changes in populations.

3.3 Identify types of resources.

3.4 Identify environments and changes.

3.5 Recognize the benefits and challenges of science and technology.

Dimension 4. *History and Nature of Science*

Learning outcomes from Table 4.3

4.1 Understand that science is a human endeavor.

4.2 Understand the nature of science.

4.3 Understand the importance of history to science.

Chapter 5: ***Teaching Science For All Children***
Martin & Sexton © 1997 by Allyn and Bacon

Chapter 5: How Can You Plan Constructivist Science Lessons and Assess Student Performance?

Central Concepts:

- concept mapping is a tool to help form proper connections among concepts
- planning helps to assure learners will have necessary experiences and develop important attitudes, skills and ideas
- plans must address National Science Education goals
- proper forms of pupil evaluation can be teaching and learning tools

T 5.0

What Is A Concept?

- By definition, a concept is ...
- ... a general idea or understanding that is derived from specific experiences; a thought or notion, an idea.

T 5.1

With Young Children ...

- ... we have limits when teaching for conception
- must overcome abstractions
- must find a way to make the concept concrete
- must avoid "fuzzy" concepts
- must provide abundant opportunities to experience real examples of the concept

T 5.2

Concept Maps

- help to plan instruction
- make the abstract more concrete
- show relationships among and between concepts
- help connect ideas with experiences
- help fit ideas into meaningful patterns
- can be used as Advance Organizers
- can be used as a form of student evaluation

T 5.3

Parts of Concept Maps (Fig 5.4)

- Superordinate concept: the main idea at the top of a map
- Subordinate concepts: all other concepts on a map
- Coordinating concepts: the first row of subordinate concepts; help to organize clusters of concepts and show relationship to the superordinate
- Propositions: linking words that show relationships, e.g., "can be," "has"

T 5.4

Figure 5.4 Concept Map of Concept Map

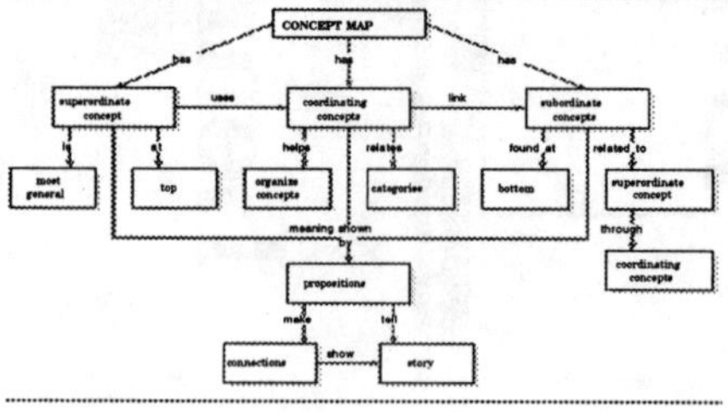

T 5.5

Concept Mapping Steps

1. identify and list all concepts
2. separate any isolated facts
3. select a superordinate concept
4. cluster and arrange all subordinate concepts into levels (no one best way)

Concept Mapping Steps, continued

5. draw lines to show relationships
6. write in propositions
7. identify concepts you will emphasize in lessons
8. plan your lessons to help students understand the concepts and to make connections with similar concepts in prior lessons

Selecting/Developing Units

- Is there a variety of activities to accommodate student learning style differences?
- Can you do the activity first, then introduce special vocabulary?
- Do you have key questions that can be used to stimulate interaction?
- Are the lessons focused on concept development?

Performance Objective from text

- *Audience* "each fourth grade child"
- *Behavior* "will build a structure"
- *Conditions* "given plastic drinking straws, straight pins, thread, tape, modeling clay, paper clips, and metal washers"
- *Degree* "that is at least 30 cm tall, uses at least three triangles, and supports at least ten washers without falling down."

Exploration

- What do you want children to learn?
- What specific concepts will be invented?
- What activities must children do to acquire the necessary information?
- What kinds of records about the activity must children keep?
- What kinds of instructions will the children need to help them succeed?

Explanation

- What information must the students provide?
- How will you help students to review or summarize their findings?
- How can you help the students use their information to "invent" or to explain the lesson's concept?
- Why is the concept important?

Expansion

- How can the new concept be connected to prior lessons?
- What are examples of how the concept addresses the modern goals of science?
- How can you encourage the students to use the concept in a new situation?, in ways that are important to them?
- What new experiences and concepts will learners need to help them expand on the present concept?

T 5.12 *Teaching Science For All Children*

Evaluation

- What key questions can encourage deeper exploration?
- What questions types of evaluation tasks can be used to help the learners connect the concept to others?, to avoid science misconceptions?
- What performance tasks can be used to help the students demonstrate what they understand about the concept and its uses?
- How can you help students use basic process skills to develop integrated skills?

T 5.13 *Teaching Science For All Children*

Figure 5.5 Role of Evaluation in a Learning Cycle

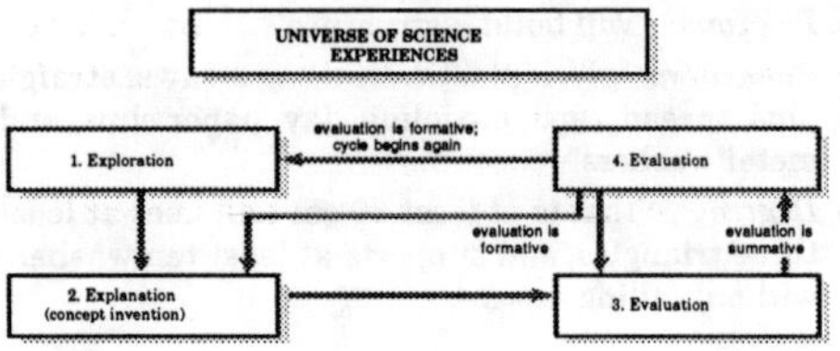

T 5.14 *Teaching Science For All Children*

Table 5.1 Authentic Assessment for Learning Cycles

Phase	Purpose of Evaluation	Type of Evaluation
Explore	Determine possible misconceptions	Questioning and student answers, pictorial assessment
	Document students' uses of process skills	Process skills checklists
	Encourage exploration	Record observations, make predictions, ask observation questions
	Improve social skills and interactions	Teacher observations, checklists
Explain	Clarify concept constructions	Group discussions, data processing, picture drawing, constructing models, reflective questioning
	Document conceptual change	Concept mapping, interviews, pictorial assessment
Expand	Document ability to use integrated process skills	Reflective questioning, hands-on assessment
	Determine students' abilities to transfer learning to new situations	Inventions, writing activities, presentations
	Stimulate new interests, make connections to previous learning	Projects and activities that address standards outcomes, portfolios

T 5.15 *Teaching Science For All Children*

Authentic Tests

- do not rely on unrealistic or arbitrary time constraints
- do not rely on secret questions or tasks; student progress toward mastery is emphasized
- require collaboration with others to construct, revise and validate
- are intimately connected with aims, goals, structures, schedules and school policies

T 5.16 *Teaching Science For All Children*

Authentic Tests, cont.

- are constructed to point the students toward more sophisticated and effective ways of using knowledge
- contain contextualized, complex, intellectual challenges -- do not contain fragmented and static bits or tasks
- mastery of content is a means to an end, not an end in itself
- attempt to assess student habits and repertoires, not restricted to recall or dependent upon lucky guesses

T 5.17 *Teaching Science For All Children*

Authentic Tests, cont.

- aim is to help students show off what they can do; assures fairness and promotes equity
- use a multifaceted scoring system instead of a single grade
- are scored relevant to performance standards

Pictorial Assessment:

- requires students to apply what was learned and to communicate what they understand
- more than one correct answer or solution
- students may estimate their answers and check their results

Reflective Questioning:

- requires student to reflect upon the lesson content and to use knowledge in a way that is different from the way it was presented in the lesson
- encourages students to use a variety of approaches to solve a problem
- may require more than one step in arriving at a solution

Hands-on Assessment:

- an opportunity for assessing skills in how children use science tools and science thinking
- allows students to use their own data and to create their own problems
- requires students to think about and analyze a situation

Rubrics

- teacher-made or student-made devices, such as check-lists, scales, specific criteria
- used to make expectations clear, to improve work, and to assess work accurately and consistently
- two questions guide rubrics:
  - » What information should go into the response?
  - » How should the information be presented?
- see Figures 5.15 and 5.16

Systematic Observation

- is guided by a structure
- observations focus on specific tasks to determine how well students demonstrate a performance, use skills or demonstrate attitudes (see Table 5.2)
- Figures 5.17, 5.18

Student Self-Assessments

- contributes to authenticity
- may be formal or informal
- illustrated by portfolios
  - purpose is to "tell a story" about student's accomplishments
  - contain students' self-selected best work
  - demonstrate problem-solving, types of thinking
- illustrated by journals
  - demonstrates the student's reflective thinking process

Chapter 5: How Can You Plan Constructivist Science Lessons and Assess Student Performance?

Central Concepts:

- concept mapping is a tool to help form proper connections among concepts
- planning helps to assure learners will have necessary experiences and develop important attitudes, skills and ideas
- plans must address National Science Education goals
- proper forms of pupil evaluation can be teaching and learning tools

What Is A Concept?

- By definition, a concept is ...
- ... a general idea or understanding that is derived from specific experiences; a thought or notion, an idea.

With Young Children ...

- ... we have limits when teaching for conception
- must overcome abstractions
- must find a way to make the concept concrete
- must avoid "fuzzy" concepts
- must provide abundant opportunities to experience real examples of the concept

Concept Maps

- help to plan instruction
- make the abstract more concrete
- show relationships among and between concepts
- help connect ideas with experiences
- help fit ideas into meaningful patterns
- can be used as Advance Organizers
- can be used as a form of student evaluation

Parts of Concept Maps (Fig 5.4)

- <u>Superordinate concept</u>: the main idea at the top of a map
- <u>Subordinate concepts</u>: all other concepts on a map
- <u>Coordinating concepts</u>: the first row of subordinate concepts; help to organize clusters of concepts and show relationship to the superordinate
- <u>Propositions</u>: linking words that show relationships, e.g., "can be," "has"

Figure 5.4 Concept Map of Concept Map

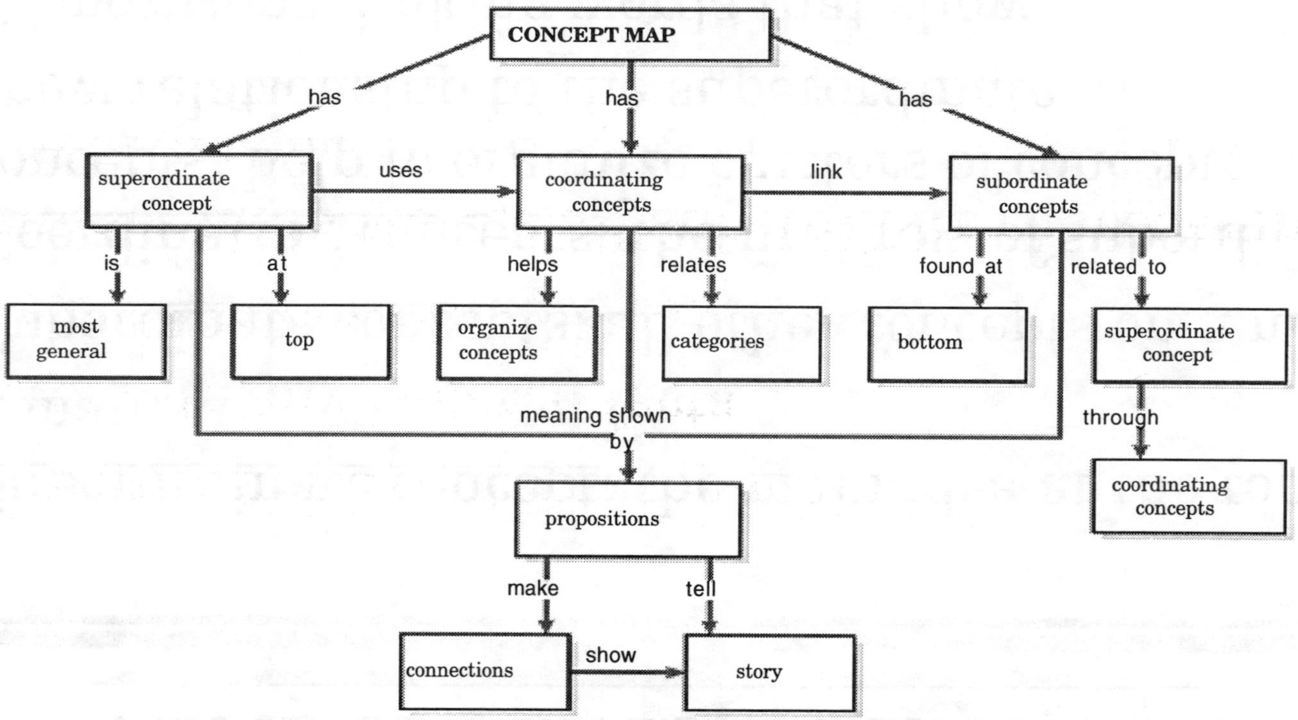

Concept Mapping Steps

1. identify and list all concepts
2. separate any isolated facts
3. select a superordinate concept
4. cluster and arrange all subordinate concepts into levels (no one best way)

Concept Mapping Steps, continued

5. draw lines to show relationships
6. write in propositions
7. identify concepts you will emphasize in lessons
8. plan your lessons to help students understand the concepts and to make connections with similar concepts in prior lessons

Selecting/Developing Units

- Is there a variety of activities to accommodate student learning style differences?
- Can you do the activity first, then introduce special vocabulary?
- Do you have key questions that can be used to stimulate interaction?
- Are the lessons focused on concept development?

Performance Objective from text

- *Audience* "each fourth grade child"
- *Behavior* "will build a structure"
- *Conditions* "given plastic drinking straws, straight pins, thread, tape, modeling clay, paper clips, and metal washers"
- *Degree* "that is at least 30 cm tall, uses at least three triangles, and supports at least ten washers without falling down."

Exploration

- What do you want children to learn?
- What specific concepts will be invented?
- What activities must children do to acquire the necessary information?
- What kinds of records about the activity must children keep?
- What kinds of instructions will the children need to help them succeed?

Explanation

- What information must the students provide?
- How will you help students to review or summarize their findings?
- How can you help the students use their information to "invent" or to explain the lesson's concept?
- Why is the concept important?

Expansion

- How can the new concept be connected to prior lessons?
- What are examples of how the concept addresses the modern goals of science?
- How can you encourage the students to use the concept in a new situation?, in ways that are important to them?
- What new experiences and concepts will learners need to help them expand on the present concept?

Evaluation

- What key questions can encourage deeper exploration?
- What questions types of evaluation tasks can be used to help the learners connect the concept to others?, to avoid science misconceptions?
- What performance tasks can be used to help the students demonstrate what they understand about the concept and its uses?
- How can you help students use basic process skills to develop integrated skills?

Figure 5.5 Role of Evaluation in a Learning Cycle

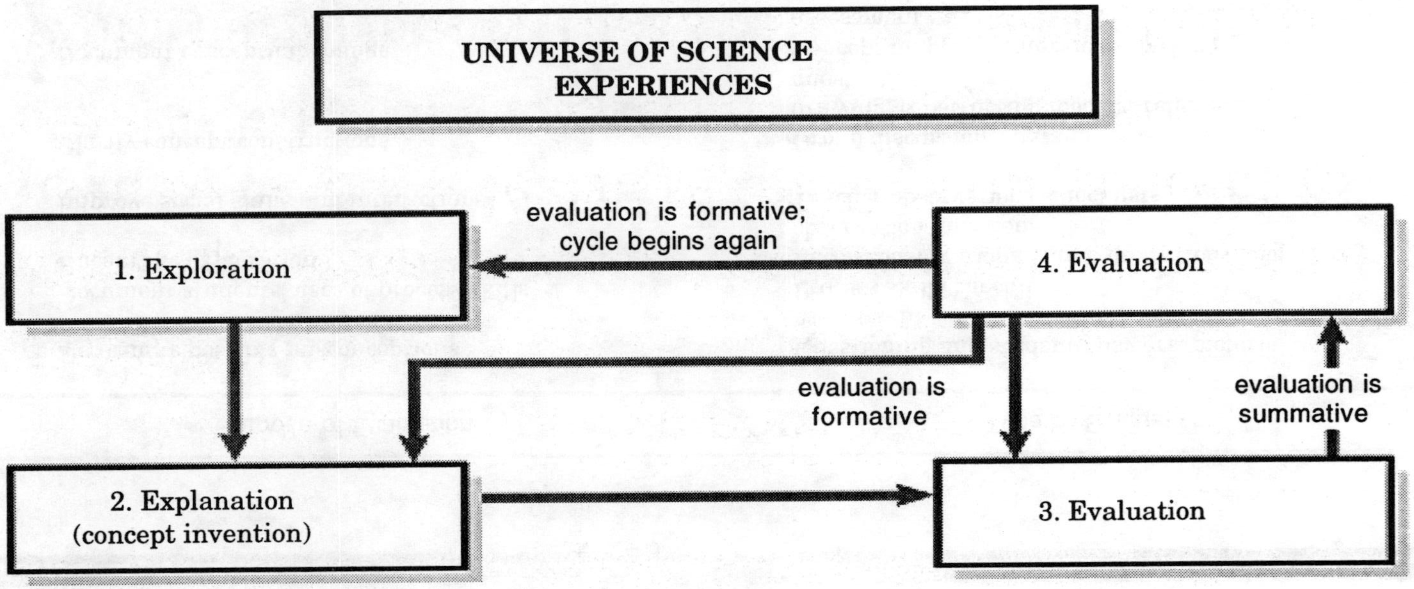

Table 5.1 Authentic Assessment for Learning Cycles

Phase	Purpose of Evaluation	Type of Evaluation
Explore	Determine possible misconceptions	Questioning and student answers, pictorial assessment
	Document students' uses of process skills	Process skills checklists
	Encourage exploration	Record observations, make predictions, ask observation questions
	Improve social skills and interactions	Teacher observations, checklists
Explain	Clarify concept constructions	Group discussions, data processing, picture drawing, constructing models, reflective questioning
	Document conceptual change	Concept mapping, interviews, pictorial assessment
Expand	Document ability to use integrated process skills	Reflective questioning, hands-on assessment
	Determine students' abilities to transfer learning to new situations	Inventions, writing activities, presentations
	Stimulate new interests, make connections to previous learning	Projects and activities that address standards outcomes, portfolios

Authentic Tests

- do not rely on unrealistic or arbitrary time constraints
- do not rely on secret questions or tasks; student progress toward mastery is emphasized
- require collaboration with others to construct, revise and validate
- are intimately connected with aims, goals, structures, schedules and school policies

Authentic Tests, cont.

- are constructed to point the students toward more sophisticated and effective ways of using knowledge
- contain contextualized, complex, intellectual challenges -- do not contain fragmented and static bits or tasks
- mastery of content is a means to an end, not an end in itself
- attempt to assess student habits and repertoires, not restricted to recall or dependent upon lucky guesses

Authentic Tests, cont.

- aim is to help students show off what they can do; assures fairness and promotes equity
- use a multifaceted scoring system instead of a single grade
- are scored relevant to performance standards

Pictorial Assessment:

- requires students to apply what was learned and to communicate what they understand
- more than one correct answer or solution
- students may estimate their answers and check their results

Reflective Questioning:

- requires student to reflect upon the lesson content and to use knowledge in a way that is different from the way it was presented in the lesson
- encourages students to use a variety of approaches to solve a problem
- may require more than one step in arriving at a solution

Hands-on Assessment:

- an opportunity for assessing skills in how children use science tools and science thinking
- allows students to use their own data and to create their own problems
- requires students to think about and analyze a situation

Rubrics

- teacher-made or student-made devices, such as check-lists, scales, specific criteria
- used to make expectations clear, to improve work, and to assess work accurately and consistently
- two questions guide rubrics:
  - » What information should go into the response?
  - » How should the information be presented?
- see Figures 5.15 and 5.16

Systematic Observation

- is guided by a structure
- observations focus on specific tasks to determine how well students demonstrate a performance, use skills or demonstrate attitudes (see Table 5.2)
- Figures 5.17, 5.18

Student Self-Assessments

- contributes to authenticity
- may be formal or informal
- illustrated by portfolios
  - » purpose is to "tell a story" about student's accomplishments
  - » contain students' self-selected best work
  - » demonstrate problem-solving, types of thinking
- illustrated by journals
  - » demonstrates the student's reflective thinking process

Chapter 6: How Can You Create A Safe, Efficient, Activity-Based Science Classroom?

Central concepts:

- educational value and foreseeable hazards for any science activity must be considered before engaging in the activity
- teachers must understand their legal responsibilities and attend to the safety equipment needs as a part of safe and efficient class management
- storage and accessibility of materials is central to an organized classroom

T 6.0 *Teaching Science For All Children*

What are the Foreseeable Hazards?

- hazards can be eliminated when prepared for in advance - such as wearing goggles, having fire blankets, extinguishers, and eyewash stations available
- teacher demonstrations can provide a safe alternative to student exploration, students can be made active observers
- questionable activities should be eliminated from the curriculum

T 6.1 *Teaching Science For All Children*

What are your Legal Responsibilities?

- *tort* - a wrong or injury committed against someone else
- *reasonable and prudent judgment* - teachers need to ask themselves if this is the same judgment one with similar training would make?
- *foreseeability* - teachers are responsible for reporting to administrators safety deficiencies, a written account of missing safety items and/or hazards should be given to administrators

T 6.2 *Teaching Science For All Children*

What are your Legal Responsibilities? (cont.)

- *negligence* - failure to exercise due care
- *due care* - duty to protect the students through instruction, supervision, and maintenance of facilities
  - » *due care through instruction* - rules should be clearly written and explained to the students; the students should participate in creating and signing a safety contract; the teachers should model safety procedures in everything they do with students

T 6.3 *Teaching Science For All Children*

What are your Legal Responsibilities? (cont.)

  - » *due care through supervision* - teachers should be in the classroom when scientific equipment or chemicals are accessible to students
- a 1:24 teacher to student ratio should be maintained to avoid unsafe, overcrowded, laboratory or activity conditions
- parent or guardian consent forms must be obtained for field trips; the trip should be an integral part of the curriculum; proper student to adult ratio (10:1) should be maintained for field trips

T 6.4 *Teaching Science For All Children*

What are your Legal Responsibilities? (cont.)

Federal and State Legislation -

- **when the potential for eye injury exists appropriate *American National Standards Institute Z87* eyewear must be provided to all students**
- ***OSHA Hazard Communication Standard (a.k.a.) "Right to Know Law"*** **- requires that all chemicals are properly stored and labeled, teachers must know of potential hazards and have available equipment to treat possible injuries**

T6.5 *Teaching Science For All Children*

Safety Equipment

- *hot plates* with an on/off indicator can eliminate hazards caused by an open flame
- avoid the use of *extension cords* due to fire hazards and potential tripping problems
- *electrical outlet caps* should be in place when outlets are not in use, especially in a primary grade classroom
- if *alcohol lamps* or *candles* are used they should be placed in a pan of damp sand to prevent the spread of alcohol or hot wax when spilled and to avoid fire hazards caused by open flames

T6.6 *Teaching Science For All Children*

Safety Equipment (cont.)

- *flammable liquids* should be stored in small quantities in original containers in the classroom
- *hair* should be pulled back and restrained with something like a rubber or head band, *loose clothing* should be removed if possible or pinned or tied up out of the way of flames or liquid materials
- *fire blankets* should be of a manageable size for easy use by students in case of emergency, they should be readily accessible from a well maintained container, students should be taught the *stop-drop-and-roll* procedure in the event of a bodily fire

T6.7 *Teaching Science For All Children*

Safety Equipment (cont.)

- *ABC triclass fire extinguishers* are recommended by fire departments because of their ability to extinguish most foreseeable products in an elementary school setting, teachers and students must be comfortable in their use
- An *eyewash* that can deliver 15 minutes of aerated, tempered, running water, to flush the eye of a person suffering from a chemical splash or other eye irritant is strongly recommended
- *Bottled water stations* are not recommended because they cannot deliver 15 minutes of aerated running water and are easily contaminated

T6.8 *Teaching Science For All Children*

Safety Assessment

- in any situation where the teacher is responsible for students a safety assessment must be performed, whether it's in the classroom or on a field trip
- the *Total Science Safety System* computer disk is an interactive system that will allow users to customize their science safety assessment, it provides forms and checklists for science activities, student safety contracts, accident/incident reports, and request forms for correction of safety problems

T6.9 *Teaching Science For All Children*

Short Term Planning: Necessary Materials

- **determine school purchasing policy when obtaining items through a scientific supplier, be sure to compare vendor prices and shipping costs**
- **check local vendors for donations, determine if charge accounts can be created and if school purchase orders are accepted**
- **recycled materials can be a source of inexpensive science equipment**

T6.10 *Teaching Science For All Children*

All Materials Must Be Stored Safely

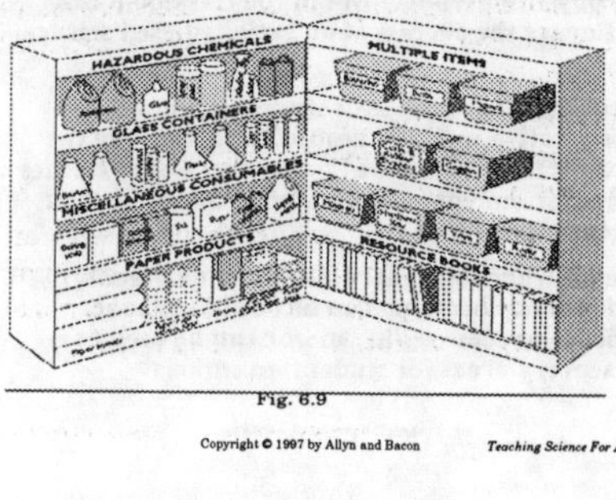

Fig. 6.9

T6.11 *Teaching Science For All Children*

Chapter 6: ***Teaching Science For All Children***
Martin & Sexton © 1997 by Allyn and Bacon

Short Term Planning:
Central versus Classroom Storage

- **central storage areas provide greater access for all teachers in the school, however they create inventory problems when borrowed items are not returned, and rely upon the honor system of filling out equipment checkout forms**
- **classroom storage provides better inventory control, however access to materials for *all* teachers is limited**
- **there is an increased chance of duplicate materials within the school through individual classroom storage**

Short Term Planning:
Materials Storage

- **while storing materials for unit instruction facilitates material collection it increases the need to duplicate certain materials**
- **labeling storage shelves is advantageous with larger items, smaller items could be stored more easily in sealable plastic bags**
- **cardboard boxes provide an inexpensive means for storing smaller items, over the long run plastic storage bins with covers are more reliable**
- **color coding stored items helps identify materials more quickly, and is helpful for the storage of hazardous chemicals**

Short Term Planning:
Dispensing Materials

- **when items are found in a central storage area the classroom teacher should be sure to collect the materials at least one day ahead of time**
- **materials stored in the classroom can be disseminated by posting a materials list for each activity and assigning student *materials managers* to prepare materials for each student group**
- **when using hazardous materials a thoughtful plan for safe disposal should be followed**

Room Arrangement Is Essential For Safety and Effectiveness

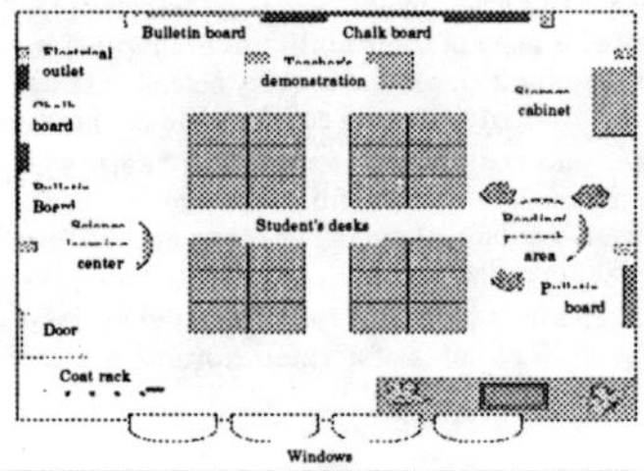

Fig. 6.11

Short Term Planning:
Room Arrangement

- **the physical arrangement of the classroom can influence the success of an activity based science lesson**
- **breaking large groups of students into small, cooperative working groups, and allowing the groups to work on the floor if necessary, creates an environment where science exploration can occur more easily**
- **science learning centers allow for individual science exploration, can be used to enhance science process skills, and/or can be used as discovery areas for student inventions**

Chapter 6: How Can You Create A Safe, Efficient, Activity-Based Science Classroom?

Central concepts:

- educational value and foreseeable hazards for any science activity must be considered before engaging in the activity
- teachers must understand their legal responsibilities and attend to the safety equipment needs as a part of safe and efficient class management
- storage and accessibility of materials is central to an organized classroom

What are the Foreseeable Hazards?

- hazards can be eliminated when prepared for in advance - such as wearing goggles, having fire blankets, extinguishers, and eyewash stations available
- teacher demonstrations can provide a safe alternative to student exploration, students can be made active observers
- questionable activities should be eliminated from the curriculum

What are your Legal Responsibilities?

- *tort* - a wrong or injury committed against someone else
- *reasonable and prudent judgment* - teachers need to ask themselves if this is the same judgment one with similar training would make?
- *foreseeability* - teachers are responsible for reporting to administrators safety deficiencies, a written account of missing safety items and/or hazards should be given to administrators

What are your Legal Responsibilities? (cont.)

- *negligence* - failure to exercise due care
- *due care* - duty to protect the students through instruction, supervision, and maintenance of facilities
    - » *due care through instruction* - rules should be clearly written and explained to the students; the students should participate in creating and signing a safety contract; the teachers should model safety procedures in everything they do with students

What are your Legal Responsibilities? (cont.)

  » *due care through supervision* - teachers should be in the classroom when scientific equipment or chemicals are accessible to students

- a 1:24 teacher to student ratio should be maintained to avoid unsafe, overcrowded, laboratory or activity conditions
- parent or guardian consent forms must be obtained for field trips; the trip should be an integral part of the curriculum; proper student to adult ratio (10:1) should be maintained for field trips

What are your Legal Responsibilities? (cont.)

Federal and State Legislation **-**

- **when the potential for eye injury exists appropriate *American National Standards Institute Z87* eyewear must be provided to all students**
- ***OSHA Hazard Communication Standard (a.k.a.) "Right to Know Law"*** **- requires that all chemicals are properly stored and labeled, teachers must know of potential hazards and have available equipment to treat possible injuries**

Safety Equipment

- *hot plates* with an on/off indicator can eliminate hazards caused by an open flame
- avoid the use of *extension cords* due to fire hazards and potential tripping problems
- *electrical outlet caps* should be in place when outlets are not in use, especially in a primary grade classroom
- if *alcohol lamps* or *candles* are used they should be placed in a pan of damp sand to prevent the spread of alcohol or hot wax when spilled and to avoid fire hazards caused by open flames

Safety Equipment (cont.)

- *flammable liquids* should be stored in small quantities in original containers in the classroom
- *hair* should be pulled back and restrained with something like a rubber or head band, *loose clothing* should be removed if possible or pinned or tied up out of the way of flames or liquid materials
- *fire blankets* should be of a manageable size for easy use by students in case of emergency, they should be readily accessible from a well maintained container, students should be taught the *stop-drop-and-roll* procedure in the event of a bodily fire

Safety Equipment (cont.)

- *ABC triclass fire extinguishers* are recommended by fire departments because of their ability to extinguish most foreseeable products in an elementary school setting, teachers and students must be comfortable in their use
- An *eyewash* that can deliver 15 minutes of aerated, tempered, running water, to flush the eye of a person suffering from a chemical splash or other eye irritant is strongly recommended
- *Bottled water stations* are not recommended because they cannot deliver 15 minutes of aerated running water and are easily contaminated

Safety Assessment

- in any situation where the teacher is responsible for students a safety assessment must be performed, whether it's in the classroom or on a field trip
- the *Total Science Safety System* computer disk is an interactive system that will allow users to customize their science safety assessment, it provides forms and checklists for science activities, student safety contracts, accident/incident reports, and request forms for correction of safety problems

Short Term Planning:
Necessary Materials

- determine school purchasing policy when obtaining items through a scientific supplier, be sure to compare vendor prices and shipping costs
- check local vendors for donations, determine if charge accounts can be created and if school purchase orders are accepted
- recycled materials can be a source of inexpensive science equipment

All Materials Must Be Stored Safely

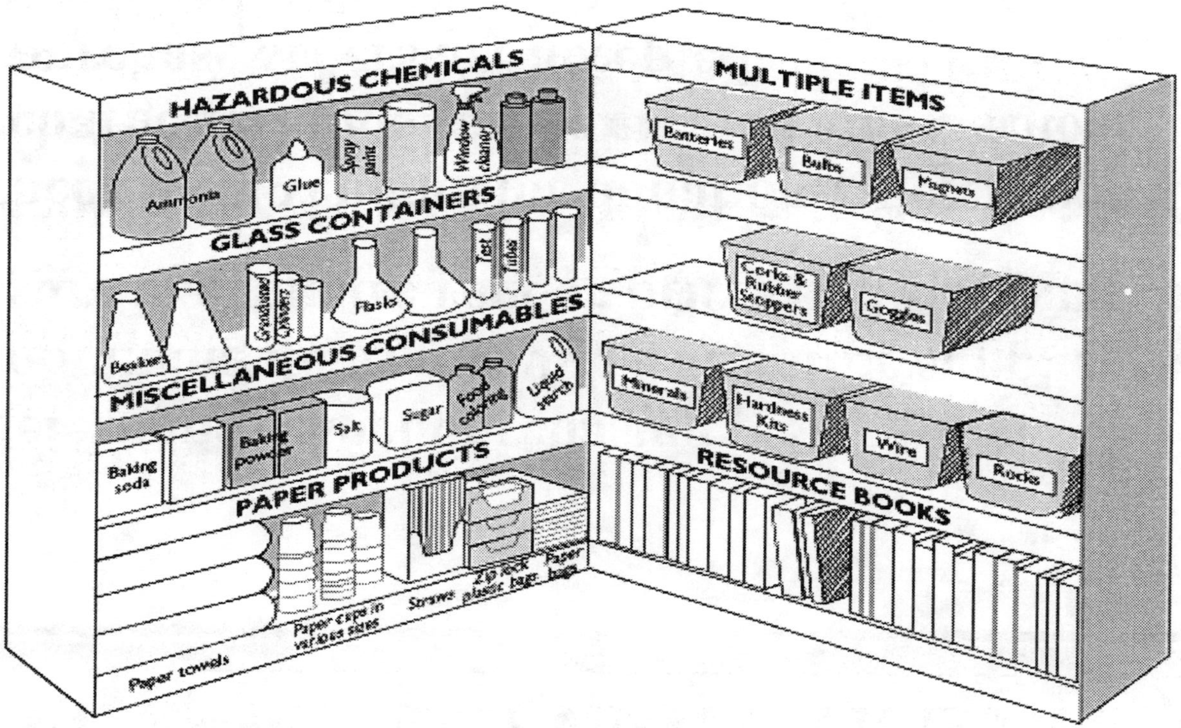

Fig. 6.9

Short Term Planning:
Central versus Classroom Storage

- **central storage areas provide greater access for all teachers in the school, however they create inventory problems when borrowed items are not returned, and rely upon the honor system of filling out equipment checkout forms**
- **classroom storage provides better inventory control, however access to materials for *all* teachers is limited**
- **there is an increased chance of duplicate materials within the school through individual classroom storage**

Short Term Planning:
Materials Storage

- while storing materials for unit instruction facilitates material collection it increases the need to duplicate certain materials
- labeling storage shelves is advantageous with larger items, smaller items could be stored more easily in sealable plastic bags
- cardboard boxes provide an inexpensive means for storing smaller items, over the long run plastic storage bins with covers are more reliable
- color coding stored items helps identify materials more quickly, and is helpful for the storage of hazardous chemicals

Short Term Planning:
Dispensing Materials

- when items are found in a central storage area the classroom teacher should be sure to collect the materials at least one day ahead of time
- materials stored in the classroom can be disseminated by posting a materials list for each activity and assigning student *materials managers* to prepare materials for each student group
- when using hazardous materials a thoughtful plan for safe disposal should be followed

Room Arrangement Is Essential For Safety and Effectiveness

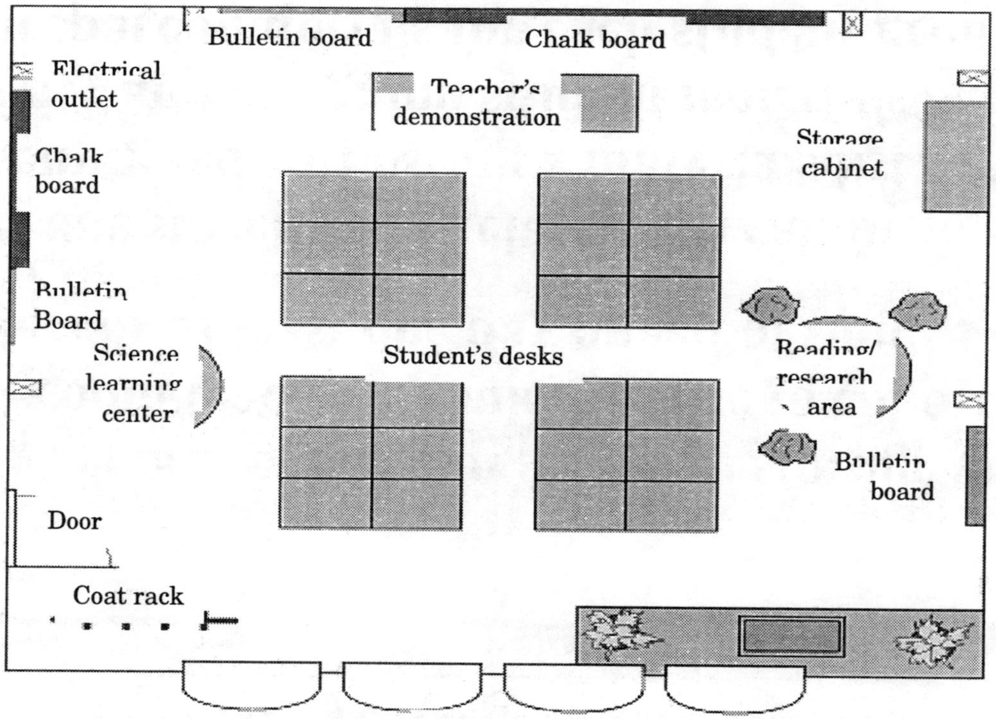

Fig. 6.11

T6.15

Short Term Planning:
Room Arrangement

- the physical arrangement of the classroom can influence the success of an activity based science lesson
- breaking large groups of students into small, cooperative working groups, and allowing the groups to work on the floor if necessary, creates an environment where science exploration can occur more easily
- science learning centers allow for individual science exploration, can be used to enhance science process skills, and/or can be used as discovery areas for student inventions

Chapter 7: ***Teaching Science For All Children***
Martin & Sexton © 1997 by Allyn and Bacon

Chapter 7: What Are the Characteristics of Effective Science Materials and Programs?

Central concepts:

- beliefs shape program development
- model programs yield conclusions about effective practice
- effective practice increases pupils' science achievement, skills, and attitudes
- supported assumptions shape new program development

T 7.0

 Teaching Science For All Children

Dominant Beliefs

- a discrete body of science knowledge should be learned by all
- science is a way of learning
- science is important for its own sake
- science affects all, so everyone needs to learn science
- science must be taught in a practical way so that it can be used

T 7.1

 Teaching Science For All Children

The Alphabet Soup

Programs shared similar features (Table 7.1):

- developed by teams
- federally funded
- based on specific learning assumptions
- depended on hands-on experiences
- selective inclusion of science content
- convenient packaging
- a different teacher role, not <u>the</u> expert

T 7.2

 Teaching Science For All Children

Fig. 7.1 Program Continuum

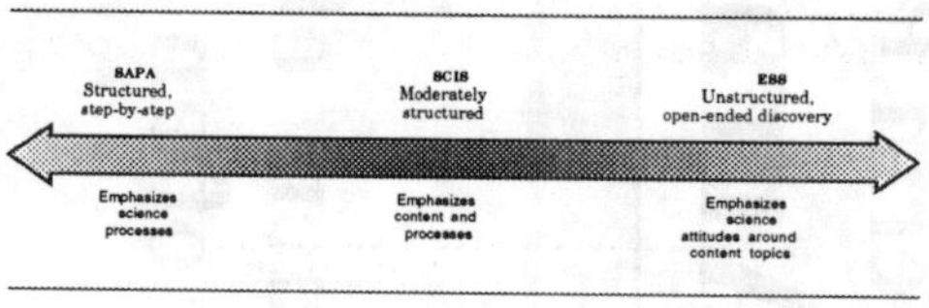

T 7.3

 Teaching Science For All Children

Science- A Process Approach

- assumed skill development most important
- highly structured, uses behavioral psychology
- developed skills hierarchy: basic, integrated
- produced significant gain in student skill development (Fig. 7.2, 7.3)
- improved gains in science attitudes and achievement

T 7.4

 Teaching Science For All Children

Science Curriculum Improvement Study: SCIS

- developed on assumption of concept emphasis (Fig. 7.4)
- moderately structured, includes content and process
- learning cycle developed; ancestor of constructivism
- produced significant gains in achievement
- stimulated gains in skills and other areas

T 7.5

 Teaching Science For All Children

Elementary Science Study

- developed on assumption of importance of personal discovery and motivation
- flexible organization
- contain units for interesting topics or themes (Fig. 7.6)
- stimulated significant gains in attitudes
- positive gains in achievement, skills and creativity

What Works?

- Hands-on, minds-on approaches can be
- superior to direct, prescriptive approaches:
  - » produce greatest gains in achievement, processes, and attitudes (Table 7.2)
  - » benefit disadvantaged learners
  - » improve thinking
  - » provide intrinsic rewards
  - » improve retention

Table 7.2 Science Program Gains

	Percentage Points Gained		
Performance Area	ESS	SCIS	SAPA
Achievement	4	34	7
Attitudes	20	3	15
Process skills	18	21	36
Related skills	*	8	4
Creativity	26	34	7
Piagetian tasks	2	5	12

Supported Assumptions

- Effective science programs:
- have professionally active teachers with knowledge of advances and future vision
- have a conceptual focus and use student-centered teaching methods
- select content carefully and make it useful for all learners
- attempt to cover less material, but have the learners do more to learn at a greater depth

The Next Generation

New science programs provide experiences to help learners:

- receive personal benefits from science
- examine the inter-relationships of science, technology and society
- grow academically and think critically and creatively through science inquiry processes
- become aware of the importance of the history and nature of science
- use themes to organize science concepts (Table 7.3)

Future Elementary and Middle School Materials

- will provide conceptual schemes that serve as content organizers; concepts organize thematically
- will emphasize fewer concepts, but in greater depth through a variety of experiences for children
- will include technology with science content and as a learning tool
- will emphasize the nature of science through inquiry processes
- will be based on principles of constructivist teaching and learning

Chapter 7: What Are the Characteristics of Effective Science Materials and Programs?

Central concepts:

- beliefs shape program development
- model programs yield conclusions about effective practice
- effective practice increases pupils' science achievement, skills, and attitudes
- supported assumptions shape new program development

Dominant Beliefs

- a discrete body of science knowledge should be learned by all
- science is a way of learning
- science is important for its own sake
- science affects all, so everyone needs to learn science
- science must be taught in a practical way so that it can be used

The Alphabet Soup

Programs shared similar features (Table 7.1):

- developed by teams
- federally funded
- based on specific learning assumptions
- depended on hands-on experiences
- selective inclusion of science content
- convenient packaging
- a different teacher role, not <u>the</u> expert

Fig. 7.1 Program Continuum

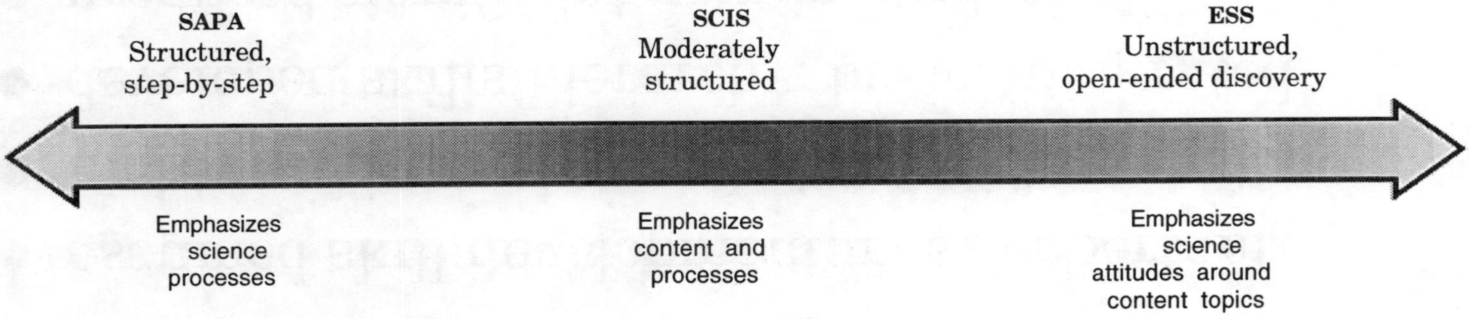

Science- A Process Approach

- assumed skill development most important
- highly structured, uses behavioral psychology
- developed skills hierarchy: basic, integrated
- produced significant gain in student skill development (Fig. 7.2, 7.3)
- improved gains in science attitudes and achievement

Science Curriculum Improvement Study: SCIS

- developed on assumption of concept emphasis (Fig. 7.4)
- moderately structured, includes content and process
- learning cycle developed; ancestor of constructivism
- produced significant gains in achievement
- stimulated gains in skills and other areas

Elementary Science Study

- developed on assumption of importance of personal discovery and motivation
- flexible organization
- contain units for interesting topics or themes (Fig. 7.6)
- stimulated significant gains in attitudes
- positive gains in achievement, skills and creativity

What Works?

- Hands-on, minds-on approaches can be
- superior to direct, prescriptive approaches:
  - » produce greatest gains in achievement, processes, and attitudes (Table 7.2)
  - » benefit disadvantaged learners
  - » improve thinking
  - » provide intrinsic rewards
  - » improve retention

Table 7.2 Science Program Gains

Performance Area	Percentage Points Gained		
	ESS	SCIS	SAPA
Achievement	4	34	7
Attitudes	20	3	15
Process skills	18	21	36
Related skills	*	8	4
Creativity	26	34	7
Piagetian tasks	2	5	12

Supported Assumptions

- Effective science programs:
- have professionally active teachers with knowledge of advances and future vision
- have a conceptual focus and use student-centered teaching methods
- select content carefully and make it useful for all learners
- attempt to cover less material, but have the learners do more to learn at a greater depth

The Next Generation

New science programs provide experiences to help learners:

- receive personal benefits from science
- examine the inter-relationships of science, technology and society
- grow academically and think critically and creatively through science inquiry processes
- become aware of the importance of the history and nature of science
- use themes to organize science concepts (Table 7.3)

Future Elementary and Middle School Materials

- will provide conceptual schemes that serve as content organizers; concepts organize thematically
- will emphasize fewer concepts, but in greater depth through a variety of experiences for children
- will include technology with science content and as a learning tool
- will emphasize the nature of science through inquiry processes
- will be based on principles of constructivist teaching and learning

Chapter 8: ***Teaching Science For All Children***
Martin & Sexton © 1997 by Allyn and Bacon

Chapter 8: How Can You Improve Your Science Instruction Through Human, Print, and Multimedia Resources?

Central concepts:

- resources are used to enhance instruction
- resources assist in making learning personal
- resources can enhance student interest in science and increase learning opportunities
- colleagues, community members, professional organizations, state departments of education, telecommunication networks, and alliances are all considered resources

Why Use Supplemental Resources?

- community resources will enhance the student's interest and learning opportunities; strengthens the curriculum
- by extending science concepts to the real world, a link is created between the present and future experiences of the learner; strengthens skills
- while outside resources require additional time and planning, they increase the depth and breath of the teaching and learning experience; illuminates the rich history of science

What Resources Are Available?

Human Resources

- colleagues are readily available and often ignored, they can expand the teaching experience
- community volunteers can provide expertise in a variety of areas (see Table 8.1)
- volunteers can help in many capacities; not all will feel comfortable getting up in front of a group of students (see Table 8.2)

What Resources Are Available? (cont.)

Organizational and Agency Support

- professional organizations, like the National Science Teachers Association, offer teachers a chance to enhance their science teaching skills through state, regional, and national conferences
- federal agencies, such as the U.S. Department of Agriculture and NASA, provide science activities, video tapes, and equipment to assist the classroom teacher
- see Appendices C,D,E

What Resources Are Available? (cont.)

Telecommunication Networks

- take advantage of computer links to remove geographic barriers to teacher communication
- can link teachers with experts in various disciplines, state education agencies, professional societies, businesses, research centers, and students
- increase access to information
- determine if material is worthwhile, see Table 8.4

Figure 8.1

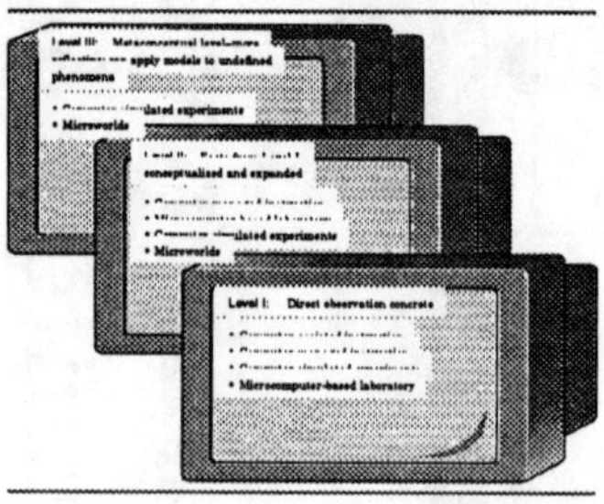

Chapter 8: How Can You Improve Your Science Instruction Through Human, Print, and Multimedia Resources?

Central concepts:

- resources are used to enhance instruction
- resources assist in making learning personal
- resources can enhance student interest in science and increase learning opportunities
- colleagues, community members, professional organizations, state departments of education, telecommunication networks, and alliances are all considered resources

Why Use Supplemental Resources?

- community resources will enhance the student's interest and learning opportunities; strengthens the curriculum
- by extending science concepts to the real world, a link is created between the present and future experiences of the learner; strengthens skills
- while outside resources require additional time and planning, they increase the depth and breath of the teaching and learning experience; illuminates the rich history of science

What Resources Are Available?

Human Resources

- colleagues are readily available and often ignored, they can expand the teaching experience
- community volunteers can provide expertise in a variety of areas (see Table 8.1)
- volunteers can help in many capacities; not all will feel comfortable getting up in front of a group of students (see Table 8.2)

What Resources Are Available? (cont.)

Organizational and Agency Support

- professional organizations, like the National Science Teachers Association, offer teachers a chance to enhance their science teaching skills through state, regional, and national conferences
- federal agencies, such as the U.S. Department of Agriculture and NASA, provide science activities, video tapes, and equipment to assist the classroom teacher
- see Appendices C,D,E

What Resources Are Available? (cont.)

Telecommunication Networks

- take advantage of computer links to remove geographic barriers to teacher communication
- can link teachers with experts in various disciplines, state education agencies, professional societies, businesses, research centers, and students
- increase access to information
- determine if material is worthwhile, see Table 8.4

Figure 8.1

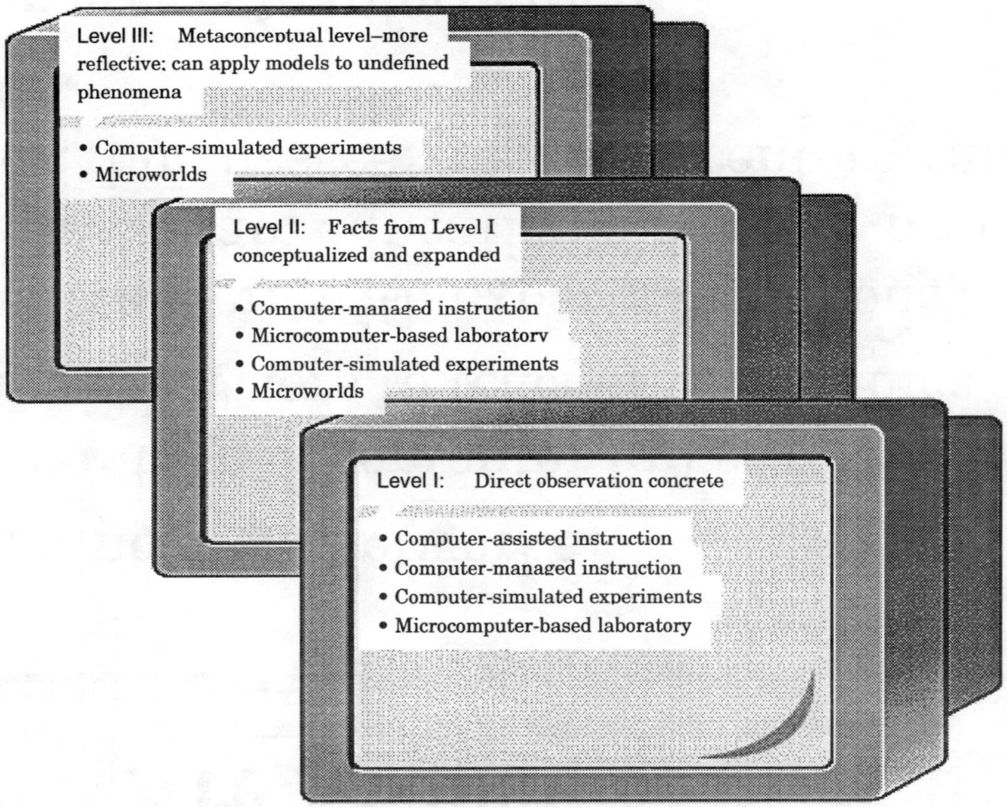

Level III: Metaconceptual level–more reflective: can apply models to undefined phenomena
• Computer-simulated experiments
• Microworlds
Level II: Facts from Level I conceptualized and expanded
• Computer-managed instruction
• Microcomputer-based laboratory
• Computer-simulated experiments
• Microworlds
Level I: Direct observation concrete
• Computer-assisted instruction
• Computer-managed instruction
• Computer-simulated experiments
• Microcomputer-based laboratory

Chapter 9: ***Teaching Science For All Children***
Martin & Sexton © 1997 by Allyn and Bacon

Chapter 9: What Teaching Methods Help Learners To Construct Meaning?

Central concepts:

- inquiry is the way of finding out and discovery is what is found
- several methods encourage learners to construct understanding, but in different ways
- cooperative learning techniques help to manage science inquiry classrooms

T 9.0

 Teaching Science For All Children

What is Inquiry and Discovery?

- Inquiry is a process for finding out, the way of making discoveries
- Discovery is what is found, what learners construct in their minds

T 9.1

 Teaching Science For All Children

Science Learning Cycle

- is built upon a synthesis of learning theories
- is a way of planning and teaching that is consistent with how children construct their understanding
- see Fig 9.1

T 9.2

 Teaching Science For All Children

Figure 9.1

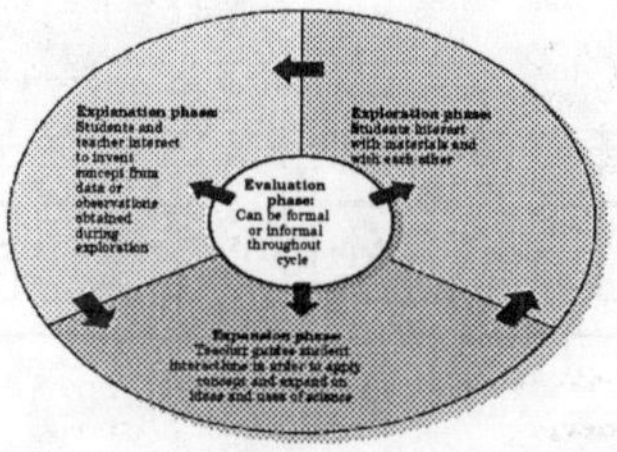

T 9.3

 Teaching Science For All Children

Science Learning Cycle, continued

1. Exploration

- What is the precise concept students will explore?
- What activities must the children do to become familiar with the concept?
- What kinds of observations and records should the children keep?
- What kinds of instructions will the children need? How can you give the instructions without telling the concept?

T 9.4

 Teaching Science For All Children

Science Learning Cycle, continued

2. Explanation

- What kinds of information or findings should the children talk about?
- How can you help help students summarize their findings?
- How can you guide the students and refrain from telling them what they should have found, even if their understanding is incomplete?
- What concept labels should the children discover?
- Why is the concept important?

T 9.5

 Teaching Science For All Children

Chapter 9: ***Teaching Science For All Children***
Martin & Sexton © 1997 by Allyn and Bacon

Science Learning Cycle, continued

3. Expansion

- How can you connect with children's prior experiences?
- How does the concept relate to the science program goals?
- What questions can be used to encourage discovery of the concept's importance?
- What new experiences will help to apply or expand the concept?
- What is the next concept related to the present one?

Science Learning Cycle, continued

4. Evaluation

- What are the appropriate learning outcomes you should expect?
- What types of hands-on evaluation techniques can the children do to demonstrate the basic process skills?
- What techniques are appropriate for children to demonstrate the integrated process skills?
- How can pictures help children to demonstrate how well they can think through problems?
- What types of questions will help children to reflect on what they have discovered?

Figure 9.2: Question Types and Learning Cycles

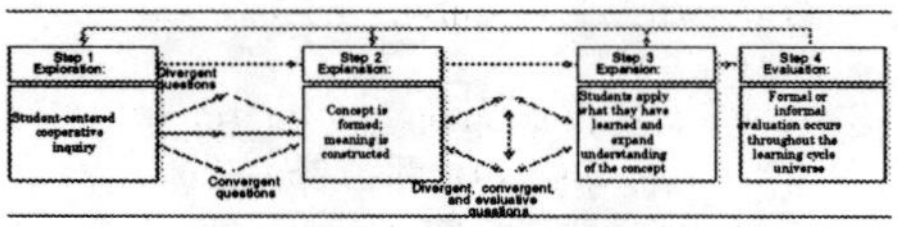

Scientific Teaching Method

- Step 1: Students conclude that an experiment will provide the best answer to the science question or dilemma.
- Step 2: Focus the question to seek a specific science answer
- Step 3: Guess an answer and use references to find out if the answer is already known
- Step 4: Use guiding questions to find out the answer in Step 2
- Step 5: Have students apply what they learn from experimentation; use conclusions in a practical way

Suchman's Inquiry

- to help children construct solutions and explanations
- based on discrepant events
- student-centered, students ask the questions
- relies only on convergent questions that can be answered with a Yes or a No

Fig. 9.5 Discrepant Event Map

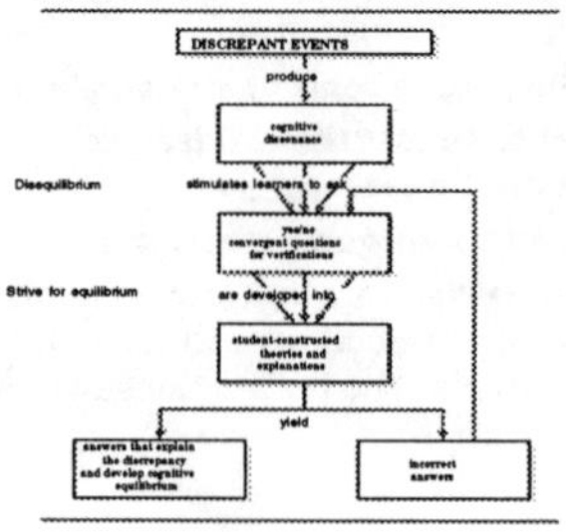

Chapter 9: ***Teaching Science For All Children***
Martin & Sexton © 1997 by Allyn and Bacon

Suchman's Inquiry, continued

- Phase:
- 1. present the discrepant event
- 2. students verify facts and collect information via questions
- 3. student investigation and research
- 4. teacher-led discussion to develop solution or best explanation

T 9.12

Using Children's Questions (Table 9.1):

- helps children gain understanding
- provides incentive to inquire
- helps children learn to construct meaning
- gives opportunity for perseverance

- Teacher's role:
- encourage children to ask questions
- encourage children to seek for themselves
- help children invent ways to test their ideas
- help children construct well-reasoned explanations

T 9.13

Children's Questions/ Inquiry Method

- Step 1: Obtain and record questions
- Step 2: Decide what questions to investigate
- Step 3: Help children plan their investigations (Table 9.2)
- Step 4: Monitor and assist children
- Step 5: Help children record and report

T 9.14

Cooperative Inquiry Groups (Table 9.3)

- *Principal Investigator* manages the group and checks the assignment
- *Materials Manager* collects and distributes all equipment
- *Recorder* collects all necessary information
- *Reporter* communicates the group's findings
- *Maintenance Director* directs the group's clean up effort

T 9.15

Successful Inquiry Teachers (Table 9.4):

- model scientific attitudes and processes
- are creative
- are flexible
- use effective questioning strategies
- focus their efforts on preparing children to <u>think</u>

T 9.16

Chapter 9: What Teaching Methods Help Learners To Construct Meaning?

Central concepts:

- inquiry is the way of finding out and discovery is what is found
- several methods encourage learners to construct understanding, but in different ways
- cooperative learning techniques help to manage science inquiry classrooms

What is Inquiry and Discovery?

- Inquiry is a process for finding out, the way of making discoveries

- Discovery is what is found, what learners construct in their minds

Science Learning Cycle

- is built upon a synthesis of learning theories
- is a way of planning and teaching that is consistent with how children construct their understanding
- see Fig 9.1

Figure 9.1

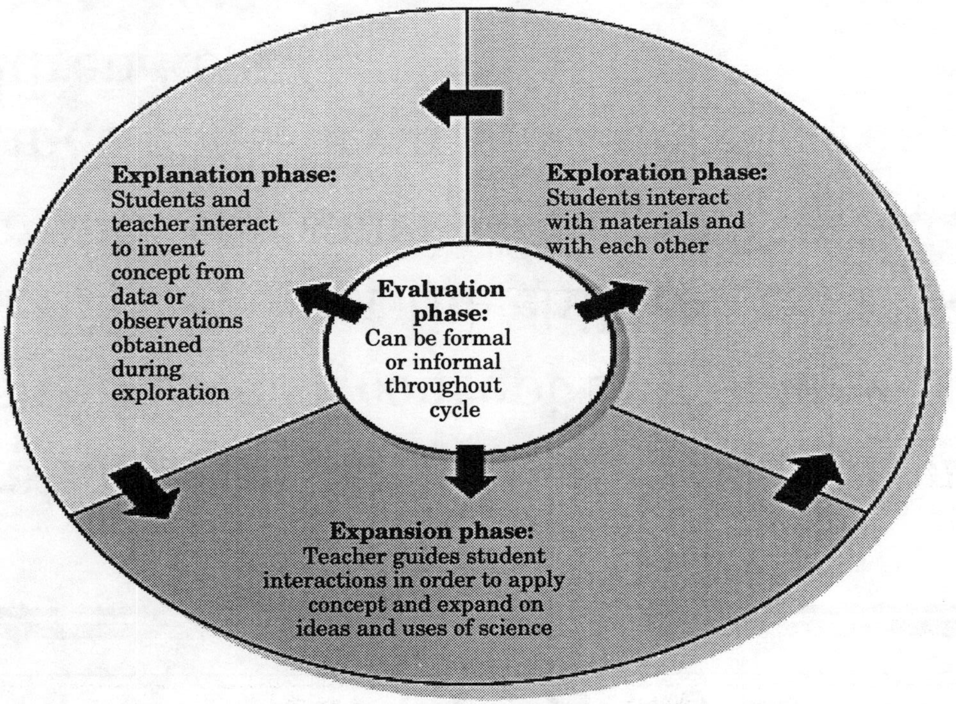

Explanation phase:
Students and teacher interact to invent concept from data or observations obtained during exploration
Exploration phase:
Students interact with materials and with each other
Evaluation phase:
Can be formal or informal throughout cycle
Expansion phase:
Teacher guides student interactions in order to apply concept and expand on ideas and uses of science

Science Learning Cycle, continued

1. Exploration

- What is the precise concept students will explore?
- What activities must the children do to become familiar with the concept?
- What kinds of observations and records should the children keep?
- What kinds of instructions will the children need? How can you give the instructions without telling the concept?

Science Learning Cycle, continued

2. Explanation

- What kinds of information or findings should the children talk about?
- How can you help help students summarize their findings?
- How can you guide the students and refrain from telling them what they should have found, even if their understanding is incomplete?
- What concept labels should the children discover?
- Why is the concept important?

Science Learning Cycle, continued

3. Expansion

- How can you connect with children's prior experiences?
- How does the concept relate to the science program goals?
- What questions can be used to encourage discovery of the concept's importance?
- What new experiences will help to apply or expand the concept?
- What is the next concept related to the present one?

Science Learning Cycle, continued

4. Evaluation

- What are the appropriate learning outcomes you should expect?
- What types of hands-on evaluation techniques can the children do to demonstrate the basic process skills?
- What techniques are appropriate for children to demonstrate the integrated process skills?
- How can pictures help children to demonstrate how well they can think through problems?
- What types of questions will help children to reflect on what they have discovered?

Figure 9.2: Question Types and Learning Cycles

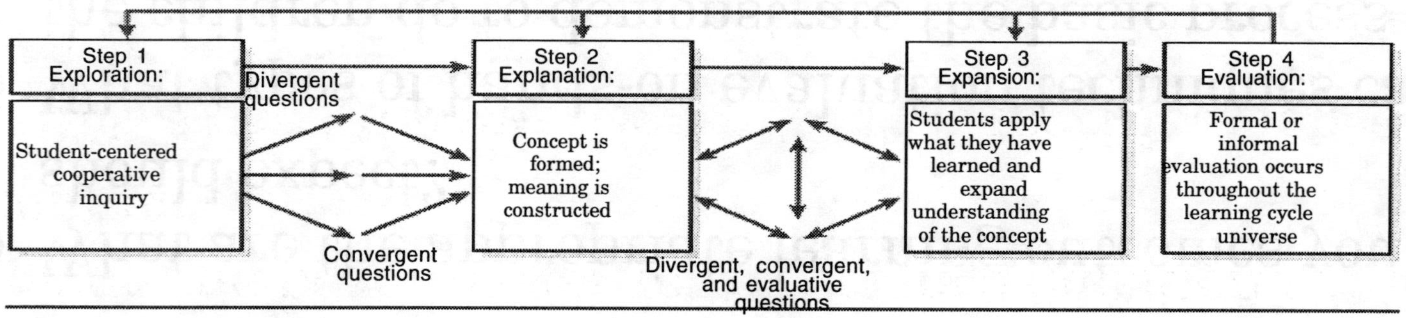

Scientific Teaching Method

- Step 1: Students conclude that an experiment will provide the best answer to the science question or dilemma.
- Step 2: Focus the question to seek a specific science answer
- Step 3: Guess an answer and use references to find out if the answer is already known
- Step 4: Use guiding questions to find out the answer in Step 2
- Step 5: Have students apply what they learn from experimentation; use conclusions in a practical way

Suchman's Inquiry

- to help children construct solutions and explanations
- based on discrepant events
- student-centered, students ask the questions
- relies only on convergent questions that can be answered with a Yes or a No

Fig. 9.5 Discrepant Event Map

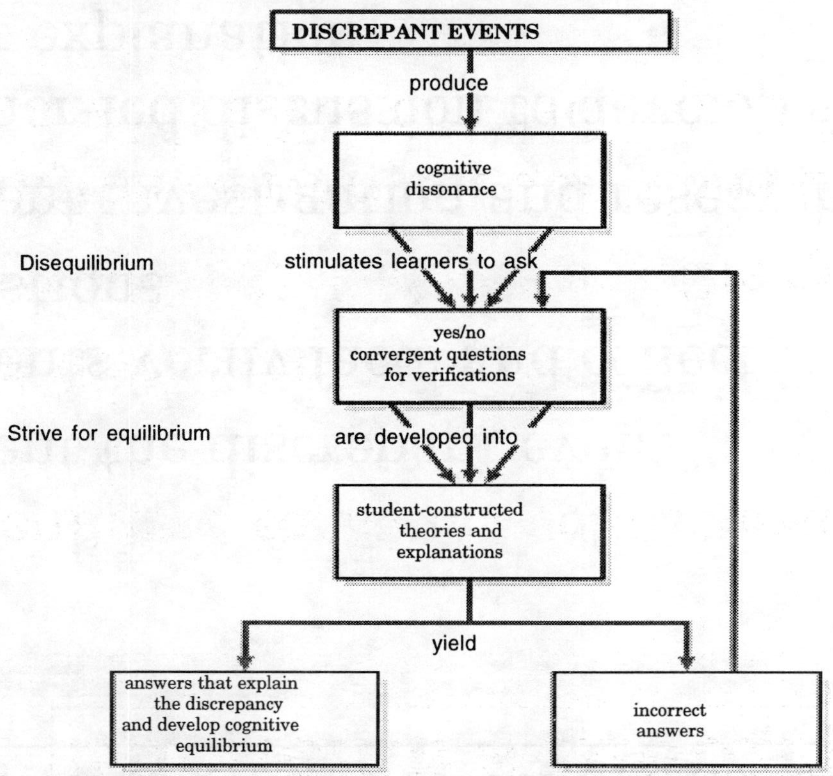

Suchman's Inquiry, continued

- Phase:
- 1. present the discrepant event
- 2. students verify facts and collect information via questions
- 3. student investigation and research
- 4. teacher-led discussion to develop solution or best explanation

Using Children's Questions (Table 9.1):

- helps children gain understanding
- provides incentive to inquire
- helps children learn to construct meaning
- gives opportunity for perseverance

- Teacher's role:
- encourage children to ask questions
- encourage children to seek for themselves
- help children invent ways to test their ideas
- help children construct well-reasoned explanations

Children's Questions/ Inquiry Method

- Step 1: Obtain and record questions
- Step 2: Decide what questions to investigate
- Step 3: Help children plan their investigations (Table 9.2)
- Step 4: Monitor and assist children
- Step 5: Help children record and report

Cooperative Inquiry Groups (Table 9.3)

- *Principal Investigator* manages the group and checks the assignment
- *Materials Manager* collects and distributes all equipment
- *Recorder* collects all necessary information
- *Reporter* communicates the group's findings
- *Maintenance Director* directs the group's clean up effort

Successful Inquiry Teachers (Table 9.4):

- model scientific attitudes and processes
- are creative
- are flexible
- use effective questioning strategies
- focus their efforts on preparing children to <u>think</u>

Chapter 10: ***Teaching Science For All Children***
Martin & Sexton © 1997 by Allyn and Bacon

Chapter 10: Using Questions

Central concepts:

- teachers use different types of questions to achieve specific effects
- questions and questioning techniques influence learners' science achievement, attitudes and thinking skills
- teachers use questions to instruct, control, and evaluate science learning
- low and high levels of questions carry different impact, both are important
- teachers can improve questioning skills

Figure 10.1

A question is an interrogative sentence that asks for a response. A question is expressed in simple, clear, straight-forward language that students can understand. A good question stimulates thinking and should be adapted to the age, abilities, and interests of the students.

A good question is one that is appropriate and is used for a specific purpose. Questions are used:

- to find out what is not known or to find out whether someone knows
- to motivate
- to provide drill and practice
- to help students organize thinking
- to develop an ability to think
- to interpret meaning
- to emphasize a point
- to show relationships
- to establish cause and effect
- to discover interests
- to help develop appreciation
- to provide review
- to reveal thinking processes
- to diagnose learning difficulties
- to evaluate
- to give practice
- to permit expression

Four types of questions:

1. Memory questions establish or review the facts.
2. Convergent questions have one correct answer and require reasoning.
3. Divergent questions have several answers and help to promote possibility thinking and creativity.
4. Evaluative questions promote decision making and defensible judgments.

How do you use questions?
How do you use children's questions?

Questions on Questions

- What kinds of questions do teachers ask and what kinds of answers do they require?
- Why do teachers use questions?
- How do questions affect students?
- How are teachers' questions and students' answers related?
- What is "wait-time" and why is it important to science teaching?
- What types of questions are found in texts and on science tests?

What Kinds of Questions & Answers?

- ask mostly low cognitive level
- require mostly factual answers

Why Do Teachers Use Questions? (Table 10.1)

- to motivate and to interest
- to reveal prior (mis)conceptions and to evaluate
- to guide thinking
- to discipline, manage or control
- to give listening cues
- to diagnose strengths, weaknesses
- to relate concepts
- to summarize

How Do Questions Affect Students?

- shape attitudes toward subject, level of thinking, and extent of achievement
- stimulate high level and divergent thinking
- achievement can improve if high levels of questions are accompanied by wait-time, redirection, and probing

How Are Teacher Questions and Student Answers Related?

- the level of the question tends to obtain a similar level of answer; teacher must assess appropriateness of answer level and encourage if of a lower level than expected
- children's language development benefits from questioning

How Do Teachers Use Questions To Involve All Students?

- to adapt instruction to student diversity
- to encourage greater involvement of low achievers
- to initiate contact and to provide student feedback
- see Figure 10.2

What is "Wait-Time" and Why is it Important?

- WT#1 - length of time teacher waits after asking question before continuing
- WT#2 - length of time teacher waits after receiving answer before continuing
- average is less than 1 second (under what circumstances is this sufficient?)
- recommended average WT is 3 to 5 sec.
- can expect improvements in quantity and quality of student participation
- see Figures 10.3, 10.4

What Types of Questions are Used in Most Science Books and Tests?

- low level questions devoted to facts in books
- about 95% of test questions are on Bloom's Knowledge and Comprehension levels
- recommend that teacher screen texts and tests, adapt or supplement as needed

What are the Different Types of Questions?

Good questions:

- stimulate and guide exploration
- include student's experiences
- invite students to explain or demonstrate
- include basic and integrated science process skills
- see Table 10.2, Exercises 10.1 and 10.2, Figures 10.5, 10.6

Figure 10.11

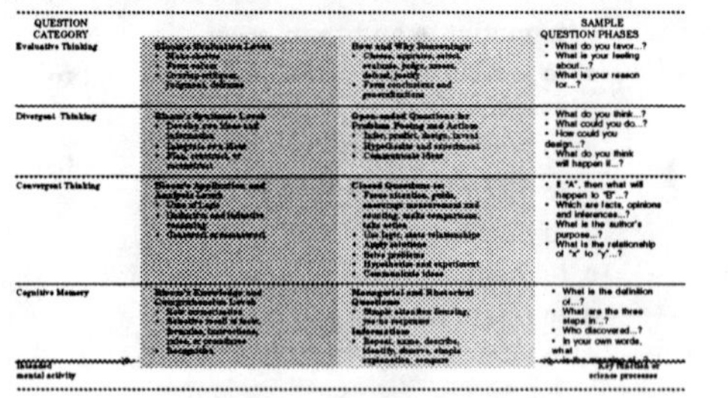

What are the Keys to Effective Questioning?

- plan specific questions as a guide
- ask simple, concise and direct questions
- ask, then select the respondent
- use wait time and explain it to students
- listen to determine if responses match the question's level
- stimulate wonder and puzzling thoughts

What are the Keys to Effective Questioning?, cont.

- talk less and ask more
- encourage complete and complex answers
- vary your question types to encourage all students
- stimulate the basic process skills, ages 5 to 10
- stimulate the integrated process skills, ages 11 onward

Why use Children's Questions?

- to gain insight about their interests
- to understand their concept formation
- to help them set realistic expectations
- to help them form the mental habit of reflection

How Can You Stimulate Children's Questions?

- use interesting materials and encourage direct experiences
- model good questioning skills (Fig. 10.7) and use questions to construct connections among thoughts (Fig. 10.8)
- develop an atmosphere of trust and encourage productive questions
- include their questions on tests and in assignments
- respond in an encouraging way and help children improve their questions

Chapter 10: Using Questions

Central concepts:

- teachers use different types of questions to achieve specific effects
- questions and questioning techniques influence learners' science achievement, attitudes and thinking skills
- teachers use questions to instruct, control, and evaluate science learning
- low and high levels of questions carry different impact, both are important
- teachers can improve questioning skills

Figure 10.1

A question is an interrogative sentence that asks for a response. A question is expressed in simple, clear, straight-forward language that students can understand. A good question stimulates thinking and should be adapted to the age, abilities, and interests of the students.

A good question is one that is appropriate and is used for a specific purpose. Questions are used:

- to find out what is not known or to find out whether some-one knows
- to motivate
- to provide drill and practice
- to help students organize thinking
- to develop an ability to think
- to interpret meaning
- to emphasize a point
- to show relationships
- to establish cause and effect
- to discover interests
- to help develop appreciation
- to provide review
- to reveal thinking processes
- to diagnose learning difficulties
- to evaluate
- to give practice
- to permit expression

Four types of questions:

1. Memory questions establish or review the facts.
2. Convergent questions have one correct answer and require reasoning.
3. Divergent questions have several answers and help to promote possibility thinking and creativity
4. Evaluative questions promote decision making and defensible judgments.

How do you use questions?

How do you use children's questions?

Questions on Questions

- What kinds of questions do teachers ask and what kinds of answers do they require?
- Why do teachers use questions?
- How do questions affect students?
- How are teachers' questions and students' answers related?
- What is "wait-time" and why is it important to science teaching?
- What types of questions are found in texts and on science tests?

What Kinds of Questions & Answers?

- ask mostly low cognitive level
- require mostly factual answers

Why Do Teachers Use Questions? (Table 10.1)

- to motivate and to interest
- to reveal prior (mis)conceptions and to evaluate
- to guide thinking
- to discipline, manage or control
- to give listening cues
- to diagnose strengths, weaknesses
- to relate concepts
- to summarize

How Do Questions Affect Students?

- shape attitudes toward subject, level of thinking, and extent of achievement
- stimulate high level and divergent thinking
- achievement can improve if high levels of questions are accompanied by wait-time, redirection, and probing

How Are Teacher Questions and Student Answers Related?

- the level of the question tends to obtain a similar level of answer; teacher must assess appropriateness of answer level and encourage if of a lower level than expected
- children's language development benefits from questioning

How Do Teachers Use Questions To Involve All Students?

- to adapt instruction to student diversity
- to encourage greater involvement of low achievers
- to initiate contact and to provide student feedback
- see Figure 10.2

What is "Wait-Time" and Why is it Important?

- WT#1 - length of time teacher waits after asking question before continuing
- WT#2 - length of time teacher waits after receiving answer before continuing
- average is less than 1 second (under what circumstances is this sufficient?)
- recommended average WT is 3 to 5 sec.
- can expect improvements in quantity and quality of student participation
- see Figures 10.3, 10.4

What Types of Questions are Used in Most Science Books and Tests?

- low level questions devoted to facts in books
- about 95% of test questions are on Bloom's Knowledge and Comprehension levels
- recommend that teacher screen texts and tests, adapt or supplement as needed

What are the Different Types of Questions?

Good questions:

- stimulate and guide exploration
- include student's experiences
- invite students to explain or demonstrate
- include basic and integrated science process skills
- see Table 10.2, Exercises 10.1 and 10.2, Figures 10.5, 10.6

Figure 10.11

QUESTION CATEGORY			SAMPLE QUESTION PHASES
Evaluative Thinking	**Bloom's Evaluation Level:** • Make choices • Form values • Overlap critiques, judgment, defenses	**How and Why Reasonings:** • Choose, appraise, select, evaluate, judge, assess, defend, justify • Form conclusions and generalizations	• What do you favor...? • What is your feeling about...? • What is your reason for...?
Divergent Thinking	**Bloom's Synthesis Level:** • Develop own ideas and information • Integrate own ideas • Plan, construct, or reconstruct	**Open-ended Questions for Problem Posing and Action:** • Infer, predict, design, invent • Hypothesize and experiment • Communicate ideas	• What do you think...? • What could you do...? • How could you design...? • What do you think will happen if...?
Convergent Thinking	**Bloom's Application and Analysis Level:** • Uses of Logic • Deductive and inductive reasoning • Construct or reconstruct	**Closed Questions to:** • Focus attention, guide, encourage measurement and counting, make comparisons, take action • Use logic, state relationships • Apply solutions • Solve problems • Hypothesize and experiment • Communicate ideas	• If "A", then what will happen to "B"...? • Which are facts, opinions and inferences...? • What is the author's purpose...? • What is the relationship of "x" to "y"...?
Cognitive Memory	**Bloom's Knowledge and Comprehension Level:** • Rote memorization • Selective recall of facts, formulas, instructions, rules, or procedures • Recognition	**Managerial and Rhetorical Questions:** • Simple attention focusing, yes-no responses **Information:** • Repeat, name, describe, identify, observe, simple explanation, compare	• What is the definition of...? • What are the three steps in...? • Who discovered...? • In your own words, what is the meaning of...?
Intended mental activity →			← Key function or science processes

What are the Keys to Effective Questioning?

- plan specific questions as a guide
- ask simple, concise and direct questions
- ask, then select the respondent
- use wait time and explain it to students
- listen to determine if responses match the question's level
- stimulate wonder and puzzling thoughts

What are the Keys to Effective Questioning?, cont.

- talk less and ask more
- encourage complete and complex answers
- vary your question types to encourage all students
- stimulate the basic process skills, ages 5 to 10
- stimulate the integrated process skills, ages 11 onward

Why use Children's Questions?

- to gain insight about their interests
- to understand their concept formation
- to help them set realistic expectations
- to help them form the mental habit of reflection

How Can You Stimulate Children's Questions?

- use interesting materials and encourage direct experiences
- model good questioning skills (Fig. 10.7) and use questions to construct connections among thoughts (Fig. 10.8)
- develop an atmosphere of trust and encourage productive questions
- include their questions on tests and in assignments
- respond in an encouraging way and help children improve their questions

Chapter 11: How Can You Use Science Demonstrations and Texts?

Central concepts:

- extensive use of authoritative methods not recommended for elementary grades
- teacher-centered classroom can be made more interactive if teachers:
  - » use demonstrations
  - » use exposition appropriately
  - » select and use texts effectively

Tips for Effective Demonstrations

- clear, specific purpose
- plan carefully and practice
- involve children when possible
- use questioning to support the demonstration
- repeat to focus attention
- keep it visible
- use simple, familiar materials
- use quality, not quantity

When to Use a Demonstration?

- to avoid putting children in danger
- to model proper skills and safety
- to focus the class on an important event
- to overcome equipment shortages

When to Use a Demonstration?, continued

- to arouse interest, important questions or to demonstrate learning problems
- to help solve academic problems
- to encourage slow learners and to challenge rapid learners

When Should Children Do a Demonstration?

- to recognize effort and originality
- to help another child understand
- to enhance or to develop communication skills
- to build self-confidence

Figure 11.2

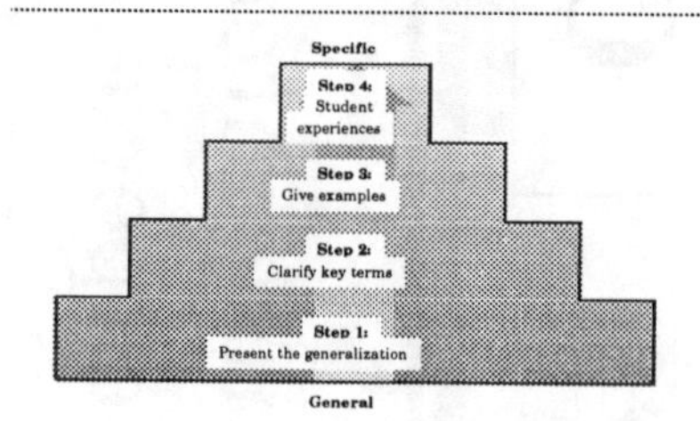

Chapter 11: ***Teaching Science For All Children***
Martin & Sexton © 1997 by Allyn and Bacon

Explicit Teaching, Table 11.1

- **1. state goals**
- **2. give overview**
- **3. present material in small steps**
- **4. give clear instructions and explanations**
- **5. active practice for all**
- 6. check for understanding
- 7. guide practice
- 8. provide feedback to each child
- 9. instruct and practice, monitor
- 10. practice for mastery

T 11.6 *Teaching Science For All Children*

How Can You Use Texts Effectively?

- be aware of limits
- supplement with other sources, including demonstrations and labs
- use local resource persons (see also Ch 8)
- focus on concepts and processes
- map the chapter or unit and resequence if necessary
- see Table 11.3 for screening texts

T11.7 *Teaching Science For All Children*

Figure 11.4

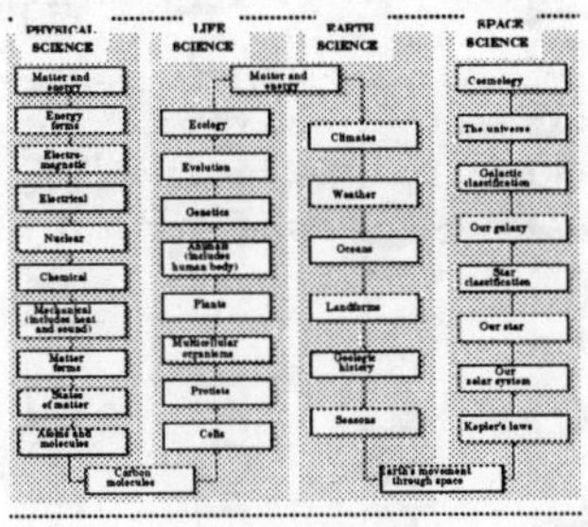

T 11.8 *Teaching Science For All Children*

Chapter 11: How Can You Use Science Demonstrations and Texts?

Central concepts:

- extensive use of authoritative methods not recommended for elementary grades
- teacher-centered classroom can be made more interactive if teachers:
  - » use demonstrations
  - » use exposition appropriately
  - » select and use texts effectively

Tips for Effective Demonstrations

- clear, specific purpose
- plan carefully and practice
- involve children when possible
- use questioning to support the demonstration
- repeat to focus attention
- keep it visible
- use simple, familiar materials
- use quality, not quantity

When to Use a Demonstration?

- to avoid putting children in danger
- to model proper skills and safety
- to focus the class on an important event
- to overcome equipment shortages

When to Use a Demonstration?, continued

- to arouse interest, important questions or to demonstrate learning problems
- to help solve academic problems
- to encourage slow learners and to challenge rapid learners

When Should Children Do a Demonstration?

- to recognize effort and originality
- to help another child understand
- to enhance or to develop communication skills
- to build self-confidence

Figure 11.2

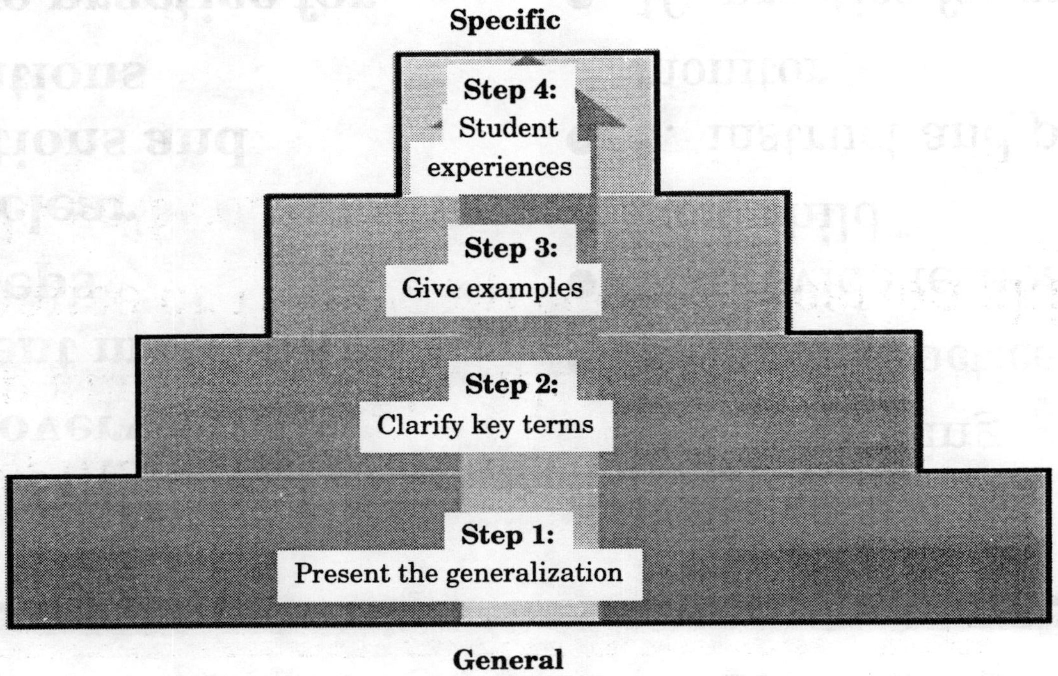
Specific
Step 4:
Student experiences
Step 3:
Give examples
Step 2:
Clarify key terms
Step 1:
Present the generalization
General

Explicit Teaching, Table 11.1

- **1. state goals**
- **2. give overview**
- **3. present material in small steps**
- **4. give clear instructions and explanations**
- **5. active practice for all**
- 6. check for understanding
- 7. guide practice
- 8. provide feedback to each child
- 9. instruct and practice, monitor
- 10. practice for mastery

How Can You Use Texts Effectively?

- be aware of limits
- supplement with other sources, including demonstrations and labs
- use local resource persons (see also Ch 8)
- focus on concepts and processes
- map the chapter or unit and resequence if necessary
- see Table 11.3 for screening texts

Figure 11.4

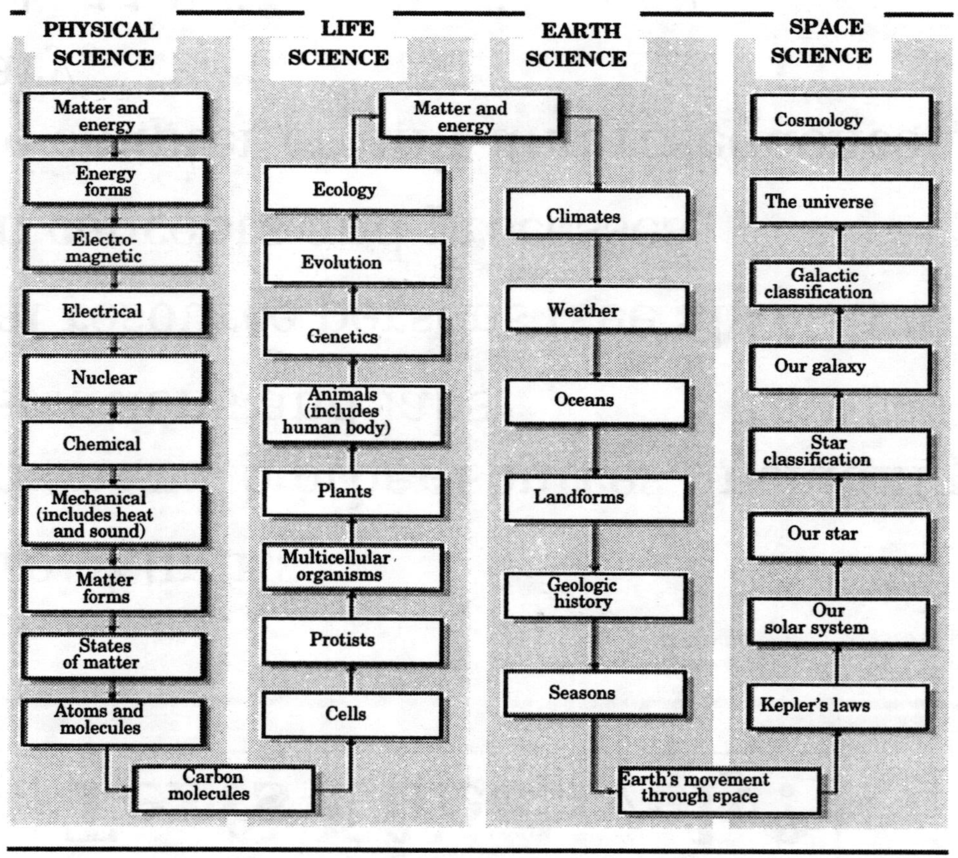
PHYSICAL SCIENCE
LIFE SCIENCE
EARTH SCIENCE
SPACE SCIENCE
Matter and energy
Energy forms
Electro-magnetic
Electrical
Nuclear
Chemical
Mechanical (includes heat and sound)
Matter forms
States of matter
Atoms and molecules
Carbon molecules
Cells
Protists
Multicellular organisms
Plants
Animals (includes human body)
Genetics
Evolution
Ecology
Matter and energy
Climates
Weather
Oceans
Landforms
Geologic history
Seasons
Earth's movement through space
Kepler's laws
Our solar system
Our star
Star classification
Our galaxy
Galactic classification
The universe
Cosmology